All The Best!

Tom

Spring '24

Mr. Mulligan–
The Life of Champion Armless Golfer Tommy McAuliffe
Copyright © 2022 by Tom McAuliffe
All rights reserved.

ISBN: 978-1-66783-610-2 (Paperback)
ISBN: 978-1-66783-611-9 (eBook)

Library of Congress Control Number: 00000000000

Any references to historical events, real people, or real places are factual to the best of the authors memory.

Book design by Artist Gene Buban

Printed by BookBaby, in the United States of America.

First Printing Edition - 2022

NEXT STOP PARADISE PUBLISHING
Ft. Walton Beach, FL 32548 USA
For more information email:
BookInfo@nextstopparadise.com

Mr. Mulligan
The Life of World Champion Armless Golfer Tommy McAuliffe

By Tom Patrick McAuliffe II

TABLE OF CONTENTS

Dedication

To my wife Sharon who has the patience of
a saint and whom I love very much and to
my Grandpa who taught me how
to play the game of life.

PREFACE

I have very vivid and fond memories of visiting Grandpa Tommy at his home in the suburbs of Detroit, Michigan. He had started a business and his converted basement featured two huge wooden Amish desks on top of which were two large black Royal typewriters, a few adding machines, phones and then swivel chairs galore to sit and twirl upon… it was a young grandsons playground to be sure. I use to watch in amazement as he used a pencil in his teeth to write or type or would use his shoulder to pick up the phone. I was his 'special' Grandson and have been honored over the years to be his namesake.

There were three main life events that led to this book; first, I took up the exasperating sport of putting that damn little ball in the hole with the flag, second, I had my first heart attack so I began looking back at the men who had the most influence on me and third we found in an attic among things long forgotten, papers, photos and press clippings from Tommy McAuliffe's time (1893-1967). These along with dozens of interviews and my interactions with him allow me to tell his inspiring life story. I've tried to get it right. And besides… I feel I owe him at least a little something because for years I used to carry a folded up copy of the 'Ripley's Believe it or Not' feature in my wallet (see the pictures page) and over the years I've won many a round of drinks on the 19th hole with it! This, of course, is not a book about how to play Golf but rather on how Golf led to his life philosophy of 'No Handicaps' and how his remarkable life inspired and entertained millions.

His prowess with a golf club was legendary. My Grandfather was the only golfer, with or without arms, who was able to successfully negotiate what they call a 'nine ball stymie'. Nine balls are lined up 6 inches apart and the golfer then chips them into the cup one after the other without stopping, starting with the ball farthest from the hole… To this day the majority of professional golfers cannot duplicate this feat!

It was a different time back then to be sure, our country had just gone thru the great depression and the storm clouds of World War II were on the horizon. But this was a man who would not take no for an answer and was determined to have a successful life despite having both arms amputated at the age of 9. Although much lesser known I would submit Grandpa Tommy's achievements in overcoming physical adversity and advocating for the disabled are on the same level as world famous Helen Keller and that his life philosophy of 'no handicaps' is on par with positive thinking author Norman Vincent Peal with his 1952 book "The Power of Positive Thinking" or "As A Man Thinkith" by Dr. James Allen published in 1927.

A thread of commonality runs between all these people and published works. Tommy McAuliffe's advocacy before Congress also helped to shape today's laws of equal opportunity for the disabled. Many of these laws are still on the books today. He also always had time for Veterans and worked with the Disabled American Veteran (DAV) organization and the United Servicemen's Organization (the USO), As he traveled he would make it a point to always regularly visit VA and Children's hospitals around the nation. He would just show up and speak with the Special Services Director asking if he could stop by and visit. Grandpa Tommy would joke, talk sports, tell stories and pray with the patients. He would always say that his goal was two-fold; showing them that if he could do it they could too and most importantly just to listen to them and hear their stories.

Here's hoping you'll find the life of 'Mr. Mulligan' Tommy McAuliffe an inspiration and a shining example of a man who didn't make excuses and loved life despite the cards he had been dealt. Golf is a special sport where there is always something to learn, not just on the links, but principles and ideals that can be applied directly to life as well, particularly in the area of human rehabilitation. His viewpoint resonates even today and his life skills, positive outlook and 'no handicaps' philosophy will benefit everyone.

Enjoy,

Tom McAuliffe II
2022

PROLOGUE

"If you worry about the ones you miss, you gonna keep missing them. Remember Tommy the most important shot in golf is always the next one!"
with Walter Hagen, Traverse City, MI. 1949

I was born in Buffalo, New York on July 13, 1893, the oldest of five children, and my arms were amputated just below the shoulder after being run over by a street car in 1902 at the age of nine. I have indeed been fortunate and blessed in life and in golf as I have played with the greats including Bobby Jones and Walter Hagan and many other noted golfers who have won national and international golf tournaments. Being able to play is a gift and I remember my first round like it was yesterday…

My first 18 holes resulted in 138 strokes and that was back in 1908 as a Caddy. My lowest score at that time was 108 strokes. I stopped swinging clubs professionally in 1914 and did not really hold another club as a pro until 1928 when I went into Vaudeville. I traveled the world and have enjoyed entertaining audiences around the country from the Paramount Theater in New York City to the Orpheum theater in LA. During the 1932, full-time Vaudeville tour, I played 262 rounds of golf on 260 different courses with an average stroke per round of 90. My lowest score in golf is 82, a score he have made three times; in 1929 at the Royal Queensland course in Brisbane Australia, in 1931 with the Erie Downs Golf Club in Canada and again in 1935 at the Lancaster Country Club in New York. I came close again in 1953 at Plum Hollow Golf Club just outside Detroit.

Going to Capitol Hill to testify before Congress and assist in getting action on bills about Rehabilitation was always an honor. The game of Golf has not only been fun and profitable through the years it has taught me valuable life lessons. It's been essential in establishing the mental discipline to overcoming losing both arms and the development of the "No Handicaps" philosophy.

In Golf parlance to "call a Mulligan" is to ask for a do-over. In looking back at my life I hope you can see that instead of quitting life when the streetcar took my arms I simply called a 'Mulligan' and just decided to do my life over. Realizing as I do that success goes to the fighter and with the sound of screeching metal wheels from the train still fresh in my mind even now years later, I vow every day with a determined grin, to simply start all over again. You can too because there is no handicap in life except a mental one!

Tommy McAuliffe
The Commonwealth Club, Richmond, VA
1957

CHAPTER 1
Ol' Number 2013

As the sun began to set on the crisp autumn day in southeastern Michigan it cast the familiar golden glow of fall. It was the early 60's and Tommy McAuliffe teed up on the 18th hole at Plum Hollow Country Club in the suburbs of Detroit where he had played hundreds of times before. As soon as the driver hit the ball Tommy knew he was in trouble. It was another heart attack as the Cancer that was to take his life a few years later began to make itself at home in his body. They say your life flashes before you when you die...

The nightmarish sound was loud enough to crack teeth as the 20-ton electric street car, number 2013, tried to stop. Its steel wheels screeching against metal rails before it cleanly severed both arms just below the shoulder. Ever since he has always been haunted by that deafening sound... nine year old Tommy McAuliffe's life both ended and began on that day in 1901.

The summer passed and a beautiful autumn was at hand. It was a time of Tweed knickers at the knee, Two-tone shoes, Fedora Hats and Bowties. Everyone was happy and Tommy like most boys his age was into mischief with other kids in the neighborhood. September 13, 1901, was a beautifully crisp fall day. It was the kind of day where the sky is bluer than blue, the leaves have started to turn and for the first time since early spring there's a cool bite to the air. The McAuliffe family had only moved to the suburbs scarcely a month earlier. Although a little bit above the family budget, the house was really in a prime location right near schools, the hospital, Church and, most importantly, a 18-hole Par-4 golf course. Year's later Tommy would share, "Little did I understand at the time that God's well-devised plan was laying a firm foundation for me right from that early age."

That afternoon, his Mother had gone to 'Mike's' the local meat market owned by her long time Italian friends the Pirelli's. Being the oldest of her children, Tommy was instructed to be at the market precisely at 4:30 p.m. to help carry home the groceries. It was a common occurrence and sometimes Tommy felt like he was part Pack Mule.

"I'll be there on time," he assured Mom as she kissed him and 'her darlings' goodbye.

For the next four hours, along with his brother, sisters and Aunt Marguerite, Tommy was engaged in the ritual fall backyard cleanup of fallen leaves. He was carefree and happy. From time to time, he would scamper into the house to learn the time from the family Coo-Coo clock that his Dad had brought back from Europe and the first World

War. The work continued and soon in a moment of quiet was heard:

"Tommy!"

"Yes, Aunt Margaret?" He replied.

"It's 3:30. You'd better get washed, put on a clean shirt and get started to meet your Mom" were his aunt's instructions.

With the exuberance of youth, he sped to his room and within a few minutes he was ready. He exited through the front door, across the lawn to the gate, across the street car tracks and out into the afternoon sun. He started up the Street towards the market singing and whistling as he walked. He was happy without a care in the world and his mind was filled with expectation of the goodies his Mother was sure to bring home. She always brought something good home for her babies-every time. About halfway to the market, he thought of the golf club which he'd carelessly left lying in the front yard. Without hesitation, his steps were retraced to procure the prized golf club. Tommy carried that old discarded club with him everywhere he went at first, seeing it as a sort of cross between an ordinary golf club and a sword from the Knights of the Round Table. He had seen silent movies with sword play and liked it. Little did he know what was in store for him and what a pivotal role that little golf club would play in his life.

It had just rained and the street was thick with the run off of oil and fuel from the summer. In crossing the road near his house, Tommy tripped over some loose stones which lay between the road and the slippery rails of the street car line. Falling in what seemed like slow motion, hitting his right temple on the outer rail; a freak accident knocking him completely unconscious. People continued passing by and how long he lay there unnoticed no one will ever really know. His small frame was laying in the street with both arms out stretched above his head and across the tracks. When he started to come to his senses, he heard a ear deafening screeching of metal on metal as the huge street car, number 2013, headed straight for him! As a body reflex, his head snapped back and his arms shot forward. In an instant, the huge metal wheels of the street car passed over both arms. After a few moments, McAuliffe got up from the ground with both arms hanging limp at his sides, each hanging on by mere threads of muscle like spaghetti. He walked in shock back to the house, opening the white picket front gate with his foot and with a trail of blood flowing behind him he met his aunt, brothers and sister in the backyard.

"Oh my God!" they cried out simultaneously. Tommy came to the sudden realization that things were serious and he began to get scared.

"What's the matter?" he replied, his deep brown eyes wide and not fully realizing what had occurred as it had all happened so quickly and Tommy had loss so much blood his mind was hazy. "Frankly, at that point I don't even recall

feeling any body pain at all" he would share years later. In fact that he never really had any pain— not when the accident occurred, nor while in the hospital and even to this day—is something marveled at by all who are familiar with what occurred that tragic day.

His Aunt and the neighbors who came over after hearing the commotion quickly grabbed him, put him in a high back kitchen chair, and tied him up so that he would not bleed to death. Then as he began to lose consciousness again, and like some sort of emergency parade, they lifted him up on the chair. Like some sort of emergency parade, the half dozen of them literally ran the half-mile to the Sisters of Mercy hospital with Tommy raised up like he was the groom at a Jewish wedding.

"What will Mommy say?! What will Mom say? What will Mommy say?" Tommy lamented over and over.

"Never mind about your mother!" was the reply.

"But will somebody please meet her?" Tommy insisted, believing she might still be waiting.

"Someone will go and meet her; don't worry," they assured him.

Walking back from the store after being stood up, Tommy's mom Mary came across the pool of blood and then the red trail back to her front gate. By the time she made it to the hospital, Tommy was in surgery. They say that you can always tell how bad something is by the faces of the Doctors and Nurses when you first come through the doors of the Emergency Room. At the hospital, the wide-eyed doctors were amazed that with all the blood he had lost, Tommy was still alive, let alone awake and joking around, he had lost a lot of blood. After five and a half hours in the Operating Room and three different Surgeons, the Doctors found it necessary to leave him armless just below the shoulder socket. After regaining consciousness, Tommy supervised the operation. He chatted and joked with the astonished Doctors and Nurses in good humor the entire time.

Think of it . . . armless. What a debilitating handicap with which to start life. Tommy thought his life was over. Maybe most importantly, those he loved and respected also thought his life was finished. The accident certainly altered the course of Tommy McAuliffe's life. It was the turn of the century, and he was off to a rough start. But perhaps it's best to start at the beginning...

Upstate New York's fall color is a wonder, and as the autumn passed everyone was content for the first time in a long time. When not minding new baby Walter young Tommy McAuliffe was into significant mischief with other boys in the neighborhood. It was September 13, 1901, and a beautifully crisp Fall day.

The number 13 would figure prominently throughout McAuliffe's life. Despite thoughts to the contrary, 13 became Tommy's lucky number. In fact, his Golf show was initially called "13 Lucky Shots". A great many things have happened to him relating to the number 13. He was born on Friday the 13th. The number of the streetcar that hit him was number 2013. He was married on the 13th. Tommy's was the 13th number called in the WW II draft. He was born in the 13th largest city in America. He signed his first show business contract on the 13th. For his 'Down-under Tour,' he sailed for Sydney, Australia from San Francisco on the 13th, then sailed for the United States and Los Angeles on the 13th four months later. For some odd reason, the number has always been a part of his life. In Tommy's Vaudeville act, there were 13 trick shots. During the act, Tommy chipped 13 balls into a moving bushel basket and hit 13 golf balls into a targeted netted hoop. He was nominated for State Senator on the 13th, and the story appeared on the 13th page of the local Newspaper. Superstitious? Not in the least.

It was the kind of crystal clear day where the air hints of the winter to come. The McAuliffe's had only moved to the new neighborhood near Buffalo's Delaware Park scarcely a month earlier. Although a little bit above the family budget, it was really in an ideal location right near the schools, Church, the hospital, and most crucially to Tommy, the local Golf Course. Little did he understand at the time, God's well-devised plan was laying a foundation for his life.

After the accident, Tommy said to a friend, "I thought my life was over, through, finished! But perhaps most importantly, those I loved and listened to also thought my life was done. I was too young to understand the power of self-talk and was allowing others to influence my outlook."

The hospital was considered better than average and run by the Catholic Church's Sisters of Mercy. Like most medical facilities of its day, its institutional looks were standard: light green walls and flooring with black and white linoleum squares. Sisters in full Nun 'habits' took care of patients, and Priests were frequent visitors. What the facility lacked in technology, it more than made up for with compassion and homespun healing with a large dose of God-power for good measure.

Food was always a central focus in the McAuliffe family. While in the hospital every day, the clan brought Tommy many delicious treats: among other things were whole chickens, wine, candy, cookies, a variety of fruits, and more. Of course, he was not allowed to eat many of these things, but just looking at them was a pleasure for him. And even at that early age, he was adept at utilizing his charm and personality to get his desires. One day, a few bananas arrived for him, and he asked for one, but the nurse flatly refused. That evening his Mother paid a last daily visit, and Tommy was unusually quiet...

"What's the matter, my son?" Mother ventured as she put her loving arms around her son.

"The Sisters are real meanies! They wouldn't even give me a banana!" he told her with a red face and partially tear-filled eyes.

Mother and son talked for several more minutes, and then she left his bedside, saying she'd be back in a few minutes. Tommy was far too young to know what his mother was doing, and the drugs had made him feel hazy. Within minutes, Mom was back and again sitting beside him on the bed. Suddenly, she started feeding him bananas. She had snuck them from the Commissary tucked underneath her cape, and one by one, she fed them to him until he had eaten his fill. Tommy was grateful and none the worse for his dose of bananas. Of course, the nurses knew what was best for him, but Mom surely felt sorry for her little boy and wanted her boy's heart satisfied regardless of cost, just like any good mother.

Everyone felt sorry for Tommy, and he hated it even though he was sure they meant well. Tommy's immediate family, Aunts, Uncles, Cousins, and friends prayed that if it was "God's will," the young man be taken in death to heaven. Many thought he would be a burden on his family, with the best outlook being him selling pencils on a street corner. "Even though I was knocked out by all the drugs, I could still hear them!" he remembered. "But it was not God's will because I'm still alive and kicking all these years later. Whenever my Mom felt bad about my arms being gone, she would always tell me, "Remember, son, God left you here for a reason." A little egotistical, I know, but I have come to believe it to be true. The more I think about my Mother's admonition, the more I'm convinced of her faith and that the statement is true. As days come and go, I trust God will use me for greater service to my fellow man," he said. "That's the only real happiness in life anyway."

During his convalescing days (and really all through his life), he heard people say, "Gee Mac, you sure were lucky the wheels didn't take your head off!" And Tommy always felt lucky, "I simply decided to love life despite the heartaches, sorrows, and necessary hard knocks that were laid in my lap. Life is sweet in all its aspects, and you will be as happy as you make up your mind to be," he explained to me. As a youth, Tommy often wondered what "luck" had to do with life, his physical accident, or with any great achievement. It was not until he had grown to manhood and had been kicked around plenty that he was finally able to fully fathom the concept of "luck." And frankly, looking back, he found the accident was really a blessing in disguise and would later say, "I still would not change a thing about my life!"

The recovery was long and hard; Tommy had to learn how to operate and live life successfully without any hands. No easy feat. His overall health and strength needed to improve, as well as working without hands and he had to work on balance when walking. It seems that he had reached and overcome the first high barrier in his short life. Suddenly he was different than just a few moments earlier-he was armless. "But what can I do about it?" he'd always say to himself.

That his arms would never grow back again was certain. He now had sense enough to realize that, and his Doctors did too. At first, he cried to appease his childish heart as he fully realized that he could no longer play and do the youthful things of yesterday. No more playing ball or climbing trees or shooting marbles. In their place now were stretching routines and strengthening exercises ad nauseam to the point where Tommy would find he was doing the motions in his sleep. Family and friends considered him unfortunate, and some even suggested that it was a shame he had even survived. And these were his family members! Tommy tuned them out and pressed on building an armor of positivity that was unique and would eventually become indomitable. "Success is not a matter of arms or legs," he said. "After all, the writer Milton was blind, Composer Beethoven was deaf, President FDR couldn't walk... They all used their brains to overcome their limitations. I've studied their lives, and I was inspired by them to continue on the roadway to a fulfilled and productive life."

Over the years, he came to realize and believe that success depends entirely upon one's point-of-view, one's mental attitude. After the crying ended, he simply got mad. 'How dare they think I can't compete just because I don't have two arms anymore!' he would think to himself. Born that day deep in his heart was a spirit that became unconquerable. Initially, his battle was a veritable fight against death itself. Despite the amputation of both arms and the significant blood loss, he had indeed survived. There were many other physical challenges, but in the end, he'd always say, 'I cheated the Grim Reaper cause God ain't finished with me yet!" And he kept that attitude even when Cancer came to take his life in the late 1960s. Promise and potential are fickle and fleeting. Tommy came from a hardy Irish people, but little did he know that the mental battle that lay ahead and the prejudices he would face would be more challenging to overcome than anything he could imagine. •

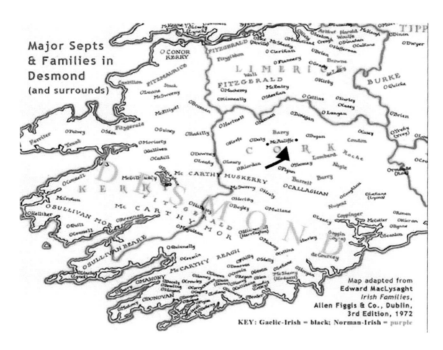

The McAuliffe Clan is from County Cork in Ireland

CHAPTER 2
Wee Irish

First noted in 1214 of Norse origin, the name is derived from "Amhailgadh," which means "beautiful willow" in Gaelic, the Irish language. McAuliffe (or MacAuliffe) is the Anglicisation and Americanization of the name. Clanawley, the land of the McAuliffe's, at one time covered 80,000 acres in NW County Cork, Ireland, with 4 castles from as far back as the year 1660.

Throughout history, the McAuliffe (Mac-all-if) clan has had numerous notable members. From General Anthony McAuliffe (1898–1975), a US Army General in WWII who said "Nuts" to the Germans demanding his surrender; to Astronaut Christa McAuliffe (1948–1986), an American teacher who perished during the 1986 Space Shuttle Challenger disaster; to Governor Terry McAuliffe (born 1957), American businessman, former Democratic National Committee Chair and former Governor of the Commonwealth of Virginia; and Pro Baseball player Dick McAuliffe of the Detroit Tigers, just to name a few.

The McAuliffe clan hails from Newmarket, a little town in County Cork in southern Ireland (there is a new 'McAuliffe Heritage Center' there now). Tommy McAuliffe's Mother, Mary, and Father, John, emigrated during the Irish potato famine of the mid to late 1800s. Caused by Potato Blight and also known as 'The Great Hunger,' more than one million Irish died, and more than 2 million fled Ireland, with the population dropping a whopping 25 percent. They passed through Ellis Island in New York that had just opened, and then they settled upstate.

Buffalo, New York, the 13th largest city in America at the turn of the century, was the scene of Tommy's early life. Two poor struggling parents formed part of his heritage. His father was a City Fireman, one of the only jobs available for Irish immigrants at that time; the only other job being available was a Police Officer. Grandpa used to tell me that when he would go looking for a job back in the day, there were signs that said 'No Irish!' or 'Irish need not apply.'

For nine years, his life was normal, carefree, and happy like any young boy. He did everything the other kids did. They got into some trouble when he and his pals raided Mom's kitchen or made missions into forbidden local fruit orchards. Ready for everything and anything, Tommy was a kid in every sense of the word, and many times his mom or a neighbor would have warmed his bottom properly if only they could've laid hands upon him! But all in all, he was pretty much a normal kid with dreams of being either a professional Baseball Player or PGA Golfer.

Overall, their mischief consisted of pretty tame stuff: from sneaking into the old swimming hole only to be chased out by the local farmer to turning the sprinklers on at the local golf course in the middle of the night so that he and his friends could cool off. "Being chased and sometimes even getting caught was half the fun," he would explain to me years later. "I remember once having to go home without any clothes at all... boy, was my face red, and soon my butt too!"

Then, like a thief in the black of night, the incident occurred and changed his life forever. They say that success in life is often measured in whole or in part by the deeds one accomplishes, but it must also be further supplemented when life's pathway is seemingly insurmountable with barriers. With arms gone never to return, truly, it was the most discouraging future a person would ever have to face. But somehow, Tommy had to console himself to this new reality with some deep courage, which luckily is a true characteristic of the Irish race. The hallmarks of the Irish culture are God, Family, and Culture. In his battle for normalcy, Tommy would need to use all three.

Energy and ambition were inexplicably embedded in this boy's heart and soul. He was determined to make a fight of it to the best of his ability and with whatever he had left. If he was to go down, he was gonna go down swinging! "I was determined to have a good life, but I understood that I would need to use all of the abilities that God had left me," he explained. "That I would never again indulge in 'normal' activities and play in the same

31

way failed to put a damper on my spirit. I must and will carry on, I said to myself... over and over and over."

In the beginning, after the accident, he was naturally very disgruntled, disheartened, and dissatisfied with his lot. The irrationality of youth had him painting a picture that this was the way it was always going to be. At first, Tommy was super sensitive and would cry upon the slightest provocation, silly when he thought of it later. Regardless of the circumstances in the years after the accident, he could not be induced to go to another person's home for a meal or even a friendly visit. He was just a shy boy then, but he was beginning to truly comprehend the term "shut in."

One day, shortly after McAuliffe's return home from the hospital, he made a solemn vow to simply bear his trial with a grin. He told me he was determined not to be one of those 'sad sacks sitting in the park, blaming all their troubles on someone else.' To that simple pledge, he would say he owes his successes in life. Not as a 'Champion Armless Golfer' but just as an ordinary guy who lives happy and successful life and happens not to have any arms. He was from a generation that simply did not show their feelings. His dad was like that and so was mine. He would tell me that relating personal matters was not the easiest task for him but that his motivation was always to help folks who think they have insurmountable troubles and feel that they simply cannot play in the game of life anymore. And as strange as it may sound, he said he found in the game of Golf life lessons unattainable anywhere else.

In 1901, Walter was the fifth child to bless the McAuliffe family. Being the oldest, it fell to Tommy to play nursemaid and babysitter to the new infant. He was less than pleased, but his reward was ample. That year, Buffalo, New York played host to the Pan-American World Exposition of 1901—a western hemisphere Worlds' Fair. Coincidentally, his Dad had his two-week vacation that year during the month of August. Since Tommy's Mom could not go, it was his good fortune to visit this once-in-a-lifetime exposition with his father on almost a daily basis. Those special days and the incredible technologies they saw were still fresh in his mind many years later. From a new Radio called 'Stereo' to a thing called Television to all-electric everything with new home automation systems, new cars and appliances were also on display. From May 1 through November 2, 1901, the Pan-Am Expo occupied 350 acres of land, showing the world North and South America's technological power and innovation. During the 6 months of the Expo, a ticket was only $.50, and more than 8 million people attended.

From the Expo, it was clear that America and its neighbors to the north and south had a bright future ahead, and Tommy, like most Americans, wanted a piece of that. When asked what the last memory of him having arms and hands was, he would recall his dad buying snacks and candy at the Expo. He smeared the sticky candy all over his face and clothes with his small hands. He would say that it's always interesting what the mind remembers. Although only a youngster at the time, he would recall the afternoon President McKinley was assassinated for years later. "Holding tightly to my father's powerful right arm, I was no more than thirty feet directly in front of the President when the fatal shots were fired," he recalled. "Feels like yesterday."

Six months into his second term, the 25th president of the United States, William McKinley, was shot as he was shaking hands at the Exposition's 'Temple of Music' on September 6, 1901. "I've always loved music, and we went there to see the electric pipe organ display," Tommy recalled. Anarchist Leon Czolgosz shot the President twice in the abdomen. He had lost his job during the economic panic of 1893 and was angry that the government would not help him. McKinley died on September 14 and was the third American president to ever be assassinated. Czolgosz was executed in the electric chair shortly thereafter. As a result of these events, Congress passed legislation to officially charge the US Secret Service with the direct responsibility of protecting the President. So Tommy was a witness to history on a very sad day for America, and it would not be the last time. It left an impression on him: that all life is fleeting and precious. The summer of 1901 showed the young man still with hands and arms... but not for long. •

CHAPTER 3
An Education

After thirteen days, the hospital sent Tommy
home. The fall school term was well underway
when he returned from the hospital. Doctors
thought it best that he gets right into a daily
routine. His heart ached as he saw the other kids
in the neighborhood with books tucked under
their arms scampering off to school, he would
recall years later. After school, he watched them
with tear-filled eyes through his bedroom window
as they played in the afternoon sun. There he was,
armless, tears trickling down his cheeks. He finally
fully realized that he could not play ball, climb
trees or shoot a slingshot as his former playmates
were doing in the fields just across the street. It
was a tough but necessary realization.

Tommy returned to school in early November, just
before Thanksgiving, determined that nothing
would deter him from being 'normal'. Completing
the long, arduous journey to some sort of
successful career via education was now the
mission. For an Irish immigrant, education was
the great equalizer, and even at an early age,
Tommy understood this. Naturally, like most
teenage boys, he dreamed of being a Major
League baseball player or a professional Golfer on
the PGA Tour. "It's a sad, hard truth when you
come to fully realize that you can't and won't
achieve your dreams. Some men never fully

recover from that and simply give up. But I say that becomes time for you to simply call a Mulligan and go find new dreams," he advised me.

Job one was to learn how to conduct himself in the classroom as well as the daily transportation of books, how to raise a hand to ask a question, and the handling of pencil and paper to take notes. "That's not really correct either because I have no hands for handling anything," he quipped. "Somehow though, it came about in natural order. You simply find a way." Those first few weeks were both painful and instructive. Kids can be some of the cruelest teachers, and Tommy had his fair share of staring and snide comments from his fellow students. It usually wasn't out and out making fun of the cripple guy from across the tracks. Still, many of his fellow classmates let it be known that this new development would not give Tommy any preference, and they made fun of him mercilessly. 'So be it,' he thought to himself; if they didn't want to play nice, fine, he was still gonna try to play.

Writing was Tommy's first big problem both in school and in his life. He was a born writer, but how do you write without hands? But words have always been very important to him, and he knew he had to find a way. Many folks suggested that he learn to write using his feet. He did not relish such ideas even though he knew others in similar physical circumstances could manipulate pen or pencil with great dexterity using their feet. His learning to write illustrates that it is true that where there's a will, one will find a way.

One sunny afternoon the following Spring, Tommy's mother went to one of the neighborhood stores leaving him home alone. A few sheets of blank paper and a standard yellow number two pencil lay on the dining room table. Being an inquisitive and resourceful young fellow, after a while, he picked up the pencil with his lips and teeth. Over the next few hours, he tried to write with no initial success. While holding the pencil in his mouth, it slipped from that position, and he caught it right between his neck, shoulder, and cheek on his right side. Holding it there for what seemed like hours, he wondered all the while what to do next. As if inspired by God, he started to slowly write with the pencil held tightly between his neck and shoulder. To his astonishment, he was able to form some letters and after diligent effort even a few words. Before long, after a few days with much practice, he was able to write well enough to do his own note-taking in class. Going through grammar school, high school, and while attending college, he always wrote all of his daily lessons and kept his own notebooks just the same as all his other classmates.

As McAuliffe progressed from grade to grade, he became less and less self-conscious and gradually regained confidence in himself. He had always enjoyed other people, and folks would always say what a great sense of humor he had. With the return of confidence soon came accomplishment. No one fully realized that he could do all this, least of all Tommy himself. No matter how hard the task or required effort, he would live a life with no limitations. "And that's what most people who are physically afflicted want... No special treatment, just equal treatment," he said. Being ambitious and not to be outdone by others, by August the following year, almost one year after the accident, he had a morning paper route in the neighborhood to make extra money. He arose in the dark at four o'clock each morning. Then, after knocking the newspapers off his wagon one at a time and onto his customers' porches, he returned home for breakfast and then directly to school. Through his own efforts, Tommy learned the value of hard work and the satisfaction of having a few dollars in his pocket.

After a few years came High School graduation year, and "Little Tommy" gathered another small victory when he was elected President of his Senior Class. His classmates seemed to like him (even some pretty girls), and he was making progress in his young life. He was also caddying and still fooling around with that old discarded golf club in the backyard. But perhaps most importantly, Tommy was doing things for himself despite the fact that he was still very, very sensitive about his limitations. Believing a successful future depended in large part upon education. When he entered high school, he almost immediately fully understood that he must make up in brain power what he may lack in arm power.

By this time, Tommy was able to conduct himself in the classroom as efficiently as any other student. He could write and was able to "handle" papers, books, a ruler, a compass with neatness and dispatch by utilizing his lips and teeth as fingers. Once the novelty wore off, he was left alone to learn. And he would later say that that's exactly what he did.

Athletics had always been Tommy's fancy. In fact, before the arm amputation, he was determined in his own mind that he was going to make his mark in sports somehow. After losing both arms, if he could not play, he decided he could still participate. In high school, he received exceptional honors by being selected Team Manager of both the Football and Baseball teams for two consecutive seasons. Running was also a favorite past-time, and he acquired the habit of running to the golf club and around the 18-hole course every day after school. He was also a member of the Track relay team at school, so this was good training. While still in high school, he competed in a modified marathon race of about 12 miles, and for some reason, he was clocked in as the 13th runner to finish and cross the tape. But later, he would say the thing he's most proud of is the fact that he started and finished the race.

From high school, McAuliffe matriculated at Michigan State University in Lansing, Michigan. There he wanted to major in Farm studies. He had fancied himself a future farmer or rancher... Can you picture an armless farmer? He could. Strange as it seems, he has never followed his vocation except in an informal way. "I started out to be a scientific farmer but wound up being a positive thinking Golfer instead," he'd say with a grin that would light up a room. "Sadly, I had to leave college at the end of my freshman year; not because I didn't like college or wasn't doing well but simply because the McAuliffe family could not afford it," he explained. Regrets? He has none. He

SEVENTH GRADE STUDENTS in 1907 of School 22, 90 Huntington Ave., were, left to right, front: Theodore Schmidt, Arthur Harris, Mabel Boyd, Florence Brogan, Grace Wendel. Second row: Fred Kamholtz, Oliver Champlain, Stewart Elder, Thomas McAuliffe, Delancy Catt. Third row: William Kabel, Henry Mackwirth and Raymond McAuliffe. The teacher was Catherine Considine. The photo is from Mrs. Edward W. Weigel, 283 Berkshire Ave., then Grace Wendel.

would often say that the most important lesson he learned while at college was, in fact, how to learn. How to go to any public library and research subjects of interest—that was the key that truly unlocked the door to independent learning and knowledge for him, he would say. Tommy became a strong supporter of public libraries and a lifelong learner. During those years, he came to believe that together with a strong family, education was essential. Sitting around the supper table, discussing various issues of the day or the ways of nature, became the norm of the McAuliffe family. Education was not just a vehicle but was now done for its own sake. Tommy always believed that knowledge had power!

College education and its resulting degree were one of the things in life that Tommy (and his parents) deeply longed for and cherished. He believed it was the vehicle to earning a decent living and being truly independent. The dream of a Degree was on the road to realization when his parents scraped together enough money to send him on a partial scholarship to Michigan State University in Lansing, Michigan. "I wanted that college training to better equip me for life's battle. In my mind, I pictured my diploma hanging on the wall with a big bold 'BS' after my name!" he said laughingly. "Certainly, those who had seen my golf game throughout the years would think that's appropriate." Tommy hoped against hope that education was to be the great equalizer and that with hard work, it would be possible to earn a Bachelor's degree.

However, his hopes were soon dashed when he had to leave school in 1915, not because of bad grades—they were above standard—but only because the McAuliffe family, like millions of other Americans, could no longer afford the tuition for Tommy to continue his studies. "A sad state of affairs in the richest country in the world," he would always fume. With tear-filled eyes and a very heavy heart, he returned to the humble McAuliffe homestead. Yes, the one right near the golf course. He felt bad about it naturally, and his mother apologized endlessly. He assured her that it was all right because he had learned how to learn. Tommy felt in his own heart that although they were very poor, he was still one of the luckiest men in America. He would console himself and came to feel that it was all for the best and part of God's plan. "To this day, I have no regrets because when that door closed, other doors opened." •

CHAPTER 4
Sweet Support

People who endeavor to serve others in this struggling world and those who accomplish worthwhile things and amount to something in life have always had some inspiring support behind them. Tommy McAuliffe was no different. Over the years, he developed his 'No Handicaps' philosophy and always claimed that his inspiration had always been two-fold. He would often say that without his mom (Irish boys and their mothers are always a thing...) and his wife Marguerite, all his efforts on the Golf Course, in the Media, and in helping others would not have been possible.

There's an old Irish saying that 'To be a Mom is one of God's choicest blessings'. "I was blessed with a wonderful Mother in every sense of the word. 'If God wanted you, he would have called you when you were hurt,' she would say, over and over," Tommy recalled. "This was always my Mom's reminder whenever we talked. During those periods in one's life when the feeling of bitter rebellion, resentment, and dissatisfaction make their untimely appearance, it was my Mom's support and guidance that was like a healing tonic," he remembered. But Mother McAuliffe also

Mr. & Mrs. McAuliffe, Circa 1958

made it very clear that no sympathy would be forthcoming. "Mom always used to say not to feel sorry for myself. 'He doesn't give you a cross without the strength to carry it,' she would say. And her undying faith that God left her son here for a specific purpose helped me fight on and to never take no for an answer," Tommy said.

If a thing he wanted or was trying to accomplish was right, Tommy simply chose to believe that he would be given the strength and knowledge by God to accomplish it. Mom's encouragement and empathy never bordered on sympathy, and she wisely allowed her son to experience things on his own first hand. It was his personal challenges that made the Irishman so fiercely independent, demanding, and competitive. He demanded much of himself, so he also would demand much of those around him, including family members.

"With arms gone never to return, truly it was the most discouraging future a person would ever have to face," he explained. "I had to console myself to this new reality with courage which is a true characteristic of the Irish race. Energy and ambition were still embedded in my young heart and soul. I was determined to make a fight of it with what I had left. If I was to go down, I was going down swinging! I was determined to fight to have a good life with all of the abilities that God had left me. That I would never and again indulge in 'normal' activities and play in the same way failed to put a damper on my spirit. I must and would carry-on, I said to myself... over and over and over."

Later in life, an incident at the dinner table when his Mom was visiting illustrates perfectly the idea of divine providence. Conversation at dinner included a remark that things were not going so well regarding putting and keeping money in the family coffers and that everyone must help. The idea of charging for meals was half-jokingly put forth by the head of the household. A moment of silence, and then Mom said, "God left you here for a specific purpose, son– You'll get along all right... Have faith!" Tommy was about to respond, but before he could, his young son Robert (my Dad) spoke up and, in all seriousness, remarked: "Yes, Daddy, God left you here for a purpose... To take care of meeeee!"

No truer words could be spoken to a father from a son. Taking care of Robert, his mom, and his three sisters was indeed a big assignment; like teeing off on a windy day, life is certainly a big task sometimes. It's like trying to negotiate around a dogleg hole in golf where you cannot see the green nor where your ball may land. But Tommy felt any worthwhile subject or endeavor in life is that—a simple shot in the dark. Tommy enjoyed the struggle despite the fact that it was disheartening for him at times. He believed it was all part of life, and the trick was to find the 'sweet spot.' That's the special part of the club or golf ball that sends an almost spiritual ringing down to your bones when you hit it just right.

"My mom meant a lot to me. Although I am the oldest in the family, she always let me know that I was her 'baby boy,' even when I was 30," Tommy recalled. As a child of seven to eight, when I visited, sometimes Grandpa and I would dance together, and he would allow me to put my little feet on top of his. When I asked why he said that when he was a boy, there was a Dance to be held after he went back to school, and he was embarrassed that he did not know how to dance. His lack of self-confidence and l arms to hold his dance partner also did not help and was a significant concern. But his mom patiently spent hours teaching and working with her son, and when the big night came, Tommy was almost dancing like Fred Astaire. While he could not hold his date for slow dances, he learned how to allow her to hold him. By the time of the big event, he had seemingly mastered all the etiquette that goes with dancing and social occasions.

The second most important relationship a man has with a woman in life, other than his Mother, is with his wife. Tommy always let it be known that his wife Marguerite was his second full dose of inspiration and motivation. In her, he found what he called 'God's true angel on earth' and a wonderfully perfect partner and helpmate.

"I can truly say that she has no equal and that I am the luckiest man on planet Earth. From the day we were married many years ago, she has not allowed me to become discouraged for one second. She has made my problems her problems. She has counseled me wisely and not quickly," he said. "She is always cheery and backs me up in every wish, desire, and attempt to gain happiness and success. Our home exudes her wholesomeness, and her motherly instinct creates a truly winning atmosphere. She is more than any man could wish for. She has helped me become a better man, a better businessman, a better communicator, and, believe it or not, even a better Golfer. Men really owe everything to their wives," he continued.

"And Don't be afraid to show affection, this has always been a challenge for me, and you're not a sissy by doing so," Tommy said. His dad, my Great Grandfather was also emotionally reserved, believing that men were not supposed to show emotions. Saying 'I love you' was a challenge, and PDA (public displays of affection) were a non-starter. My dad was not demonstrative, too, learning it from Grandpa, who learned it from his father, and on and on it goes.

McAuliffe believed that a smile and a laugh, regardless of how tough and trying the day, is always a good tonic. History says that in ancient times the Japanese were forced to smile whenever near royalty or those of a higher social station. If they failed to smile, they were punished. In his office in the basement, above his desk, was a small sign with an old Japanese saying: 'He who laughs and smiles away, the little trials of life today, will live to laugh and smile away, the greater trials of another day!' Tommy put it into practice every day.

"In my travels around the world, people have always praised me for what I was able to do with a golf club, but the real credit belongs to my mom and my wife. It was their faith, hope, tenacity, and womanly resourcefulness that made all the difference in my life," he asserted. "I hope you'll be fortunate enough to have the support of having a similar caddy in your corner as it makes a world of difference," he related.

With a solid family behind him, a love of language, and the motivation of necessity, it was time to make some money, and Tommy got after the American dream. •

Dapper Duds in 1927

CHAPTER 5
News Hound

Reporter and News Anchor Edward R Murrow was a hero of Tommy's. Being a public servant to disseminate the news of the day or cover the sports we love was one of life's highest callings to him. And to be a journalist, operating a typewriter was essential. Tommy purchased his first professional typewriter—a Deluxe Royal—in the mid-1930s. Before that, he was held a pencil in his mouth and wrote notes. But even using a modern typewriter, it was letter by letter, word by word. And if you want a copy of the document...

He solved the seemingly impossible problem of operating a typewriter by using an ordinary pencil with a large eraser on one end with which the keys are hit and the carriage moved. The other end is held between his lips and teeth. After years of practice, he could type accurately at about thirty-five words per minute. To rip the paper feed off the AP/UPI wire machines, one could see young Tommy run by the machines, grab the end of the roll under his chin, and rip it off, taking it to the Copy Desk. He loved the hustle and bustle of the Newsroom and the day he got his first by-line, it was a holiday at the McAuliffe household.

His time in the media was not just in the back of the camera or typewriter, but as a performer, he would also be regularly interviewed by the press. "In my travels around the world, I've had many interesting interviews, and it was while playing the Paramount Theater in New York City that I was interviewed by national NBC Radio," he recalled. "I tried to explain to the interviewer and the radio audience that I do not consider myself to be special. I merely refuse to be defeated by the loss of a couple of arms, and I'm determined to fully use what God has left me— my brains and my two good legs. And that most importantly, every hardship can be overcome with a good mental attitude," he asserted. In proving he had no handicaps, he found that the battle is usually within. In learning to do the impossible... Playing golf, operating a typewriter, or just living life with no hands... he believes he has proven his 'No Handicaps' philosophy by direct experience. Tommy would often say that when they amputated his arms, it was lucky they didn't amputate his brain. He shows us that someone who uses all they have will always be more than folks who rest upon their abilities.

Tommy learned to type 35wpm one key at a time!

McAuliffe started his journalism career as a junior reporter and worked the news desk overnight at The Buffalo News Journal. The ambitious young reporter worked in the Newsroom with bourbon and smoke covering everything from dog bites to fires to robberies and murders. Tommy's ability to get folks to open up for an interview (having no arms does have some advantages) was an excellent tool as a journalist. Perhaps due to his infirmity, folks would let their guard down and tell him stuff they would never say to a regular reporter. Additionally, Tommy's connections with the police and fire departments proved very helpful. It got to the point where the dispatchers would call him right after broadcasting the call to the officers or firefighters in the field. So many times, Tommy would get the scoop and be at the fire or scene of the crime long before his competitors, which was something that his editors naturally took notice of. But hard news was not his passion, and his hard work paid off. Soon Tommy was promoted and got to work on the newspaper's Sports Page and eventually became its Golf Editor. His pay was $17 a week. His time on the course and his inroads with the greatest golfers of the time made him an asset to both publisher- and reader-alike. The thirteen and a half years covering golf in the media were golden. "Through reporting on golf, I have met most of the golf greats, including Bobby Jones from Atlanta, Walter Hagan from Detroit, Jim Dowdy from Los Angeles, and trick shot golfer Joe Kirkwood from New York, just to name a few," he said.

Later, he was instrumental in establishing the Buffalo Sports Association (which helped bring the Buffalo Bills NFL football team to town) as well as supporting local sports teams and programs for kids. They also tried to bring the 1948 Summer Olympics to Buffalo and upstate New York, but the city was beaten out by London, England.

He was outspoken and had editorials on handicap rights published in many major US newspapers. Tommy was a lifelong Democrat and believed that citizens must be involved if democracy was to work. He was always disappointed that he could not serve in defending America, so he tried to help in other ways. He firmly believed that the handicapped, especially Veterans, were due a helping hand not out of charity but because it was just good business and

profitable. His editorials and letters to the editor promoted the idea that the disabled didn't want handouts, just equal protection and opportunity under the law. This was at a time in America when those who were missing a limb, blind, or deaf were thought of as 'less than,' and Tommy felt the press had an obligation to cover their struggle. His op-eds were also frequently humorous and pointed.

Seeing a need for the disabled community to have a publication, in 1934, he created Crutch & Cane Magazine. It was a bi-monthly magazine for the handicapped, featuring useful articles about living with various limitations as well as articles about how government policies and proposals might affect those with disabilities. The magazine had thousands of subscribers worldwide and was published for more than twenty-five years until 1955.

Tommy was also featured on television in various movie newsreels and most notably on a popular TV show called 'You Asked for It,' hosted by Art Baker on ABC and 'This is Your Life' with Ralph Edwards on CBS. Another honor that helped spread his story around the world was him being featured in 'Ripley's Believe It or Not' twice— once in 1956 and again in 2013. Suffice to say that in addition to writing, Mr. Mulligan enjoyed the spotlight and helping others by sharing his story and some golf tricks. He continued to write various articles and a yet-to-be-published book, "No Handicaps" until he died... all done one key at a time via the pencil and his mouth. •

CHAPTER 6
Fore!

To the day he died, Tommy's interest and activity in the sport Golf were only exceeded by his interest in the work of improving the lives of others. It was the 1930s, and Golf was more popular than ever. It was Tommy's new field of dreams. He had been a 'Looper' (the old name for Caddy) during his newspaper delivery days, and he had watched golfers thru the fence at the local golf course since the time he could leave his back yard. 'Yeah, but how?' he would always ask himself. Think of it, an armless young man trying to play the most exasperating game in the world. He thought about it, watched others do it, and prayed about it for a very long time. To be close to the game and make a little money, he again began carrying the clubs of others as often as he could. And over time, he learned not just the mechanics of the game but the etiquette and sportsmanship of it as well. And whether on the Golf Course or doing a show or at a press interview, Tommy was always impeccably dressed and cleanly pressed. It was either a full double-breasted suit with pleated cuffed pants or a freshly laundered, starched super white short sleeve cotton shirt with tweed knee-knickers topped off with round wire-rim glasses and his black sweptback hair.

During his world travels later, Tommy McAuliffe was often introduced as "World Champion Armless Golfer" when about to play or talk to some organization or civic club. The remark is a little tongue in cheek as, naturally, there really is no championship tournament for armless Golfers. But the introduction caused amazement, and the facial expressions of his audiences always said, "We don't believe it." Tommy didn't blame them in the least. His scrapbooks prove that better than 98 percent of the sports writers, editors, and feature writers who have written about him through the years and the intros at his personal appearances worldwide have used the word 'unbelievable' at one point or another. Further, they might say something like, "The ancient game of golf is indeed tough enough to play passingly well with two good arms, but to play it without them, well, that's something special." It certainly was.

Living across the street from a Golf Course was very handy, and Tommy soon became a regular and one of the most popular caddies. His heart and soul were soon fully into this new sport. One day after carrying clubs for an impressive 218 holes or 7 rounds, he found an old discarded 7iron golf club in the outgoing trash. He took it, and he could not be separated from that club for the next year and a half. After school, he would run to the golf club, a distance of nearly 4 miles, where he continued to develop a deep love and keen insight for the game. He was able to caddy with only a few challenges. The bag was put on his right shoulder, and his player/employer simply took his own clubs from the bag and then put them back. Sort of a self-serve club selection approach. Tommy soon learned that the essentials of a good looper were not really the toting of the bag and being able to hand out the clubs, but the ability to read the lay of green, the distance to the hole, the direction of the wind, and then, of course, to find that little white ball after it was hit. Luckily he had good eyesight.

But Tommy's player's heart ached hard each day as he watched his fellow caddies playing golf on the improvised course next to the caddy and golf shop. He longed to be able to swing a golf club and hit the ball the way others did. He caught himself saying internally over and over again, "How can you play golf if you have no arms?" And he vowed to himself to change that to a positive affirmation of 'I can play.' As days passed, he gradually consoled himself that he would have to be satisfied with being just a caddy and what he termed 'a golf wallflower'. The more he thought about it, frankly, the angrier he got. And the more he thought about it, the more determined he became. He would play someday and somehow. Determination turned into action, and he became inseparable from that little old golf club. He finally figured that if he could write by holding a pen or pencil between his neck and shoulder, there should be no real reason why he shouldn't be able to hold a club and play golf in the very same manner. And he did.

With some difficulty, he began working with the discarded golf club everywhere: at the rear of the Caddy clubhouse, in the backyard, at the park—everywhere and every day. He also started experimenting in his bedroom at night. He would turn on the radio and bounce the ball on the head of the club to the beat of the music. Practice enabled Tommy to control the club's swing and hit the ball solidly. At first, the aim was just a few feet. With a firm hope, he practiced day after day. Repetition towards perfection was the thought. He practiced and practiced until he mastered the art of hitting the ball straight. Then he worked on hitting it for a reasonable and respectable distance, about 100-150 yards.

With these accomplishments, he was suddenly the proudest and happiest kid in the neighborhood. Now he might be able to at least play with his pals on the improvised caddy golf course. No longer would he have to console himself over being a wallflower in the game of golf he came to love. Now he could actually play, and play is what he did. And after a while, he started sinking the ball with sheer will and an almost invisible psychic power as his balls rolled along the fairway and the green towards the hole.

One day, summoning up a sufficient amount of courage and with the course being closed to the public, he decided to play a round on the full public course, the same 18-holes over which he had trampled hundreds of miles as a club toter. Like all players when they play a course for the first time, he was nervous. He had borrowed enough clubs to play, and word got around. Soon folks started to gather to watch. You can picture the amazement of onlookers when the young looper teed off for the first hole. Records show that he required nine strokes for this 365-yard hole. He cared little about the scores at first; he was now in seventh heaven because he was actually able to play. The young ball-striker required 139 strokes to play that first round, but the idea that he finished soon became the talk of the town, well as least in their neighborhood.

Tommy's progress at golf was slow at first, but it was not long until he had the gumption to compete in the annual Caddy Golf Championship for the attractive prizes donated by club members. The competition was fierce, but it was his good fortune to win this championship not just once but twice in 1911 and 1912. His game advanced to the point where he could negotiate the challenging Country Club 18 holes in only 108 strokes. Par was 72. This is not a remarkable score as scores go, but it made him very proud and rightly so. Only about 80 percent of golfers with both arms are capable of playing 18 holes in only 108 strokes. He was only 15 when he achieved and recorded his first par score. Tommy was doing the seemingly impossible, and in a time when folks were depressed and feeling down, it felt good to him to "give folks some fun and entertainment if only for a little while."

1932 saw Tommy McAuliffe playing the incredible 262 rounds of golf on almost as many golf courses across America. He had an average score per round of 92. Over the years, he traveled nearly 1,000,000 miles, playing golf for thousands of spectators. In 1935, he hit a golf ball approximately 319,000 times in one year, and that same year he chipped 283 golf balls into a basket from 25 yards away without missing. "I was not trying to impress folks, just get them to have some fun and listen to the message. I can tell you without hesitation that the lessons learned later in life are the same ones I learned early on at the golf course," he maintained.

A nickname that never stuck was 'Tommy the Train' because as he walked down the fairway, he'd be smoking one of his Lucky Strike cigarettes, and he looked like a train locomotive. His swing was body-driven by necessity and was compared to that of golfing great Ben Hogan—a smooth pivot at the waist and flex at the knees resulted in a great golf swing and a solid ball connection. His swing has ramifications that last to this day. He became a golf purist. You play it where it lies, abide by rules, with proper dress and etiquette being observed at all times. His excessive play at times came at a physical cost to his back and knees, so much so that later in life, he would need a day after to recuperate.

In 1927, when the local district sports association was formed, Tommy was elected its First Secretary and served in that capacity for nine years. While serving as Secretary to help sports grow in the Buffalo area, he was also attached to the Buffalo News as its golf reporter/editor. One of the great perks of working at the paper was

Tommy's yearly pleasure of covering the National Golf Championship and US Open. The years of rubbing elbows with the golf giants of the day would be a great help to Tommy later in life. "Those assignments will forever be cherished by me, and as I look back upon them, it was proper schooling of the practical kind from the best strikers on the planet. The fourteen years of covering golf in the media were golden for me," he said.

Through reporting on golf, Tommy met most of the greats of the golden age of golf. He was easy to like and developed close relationships with Olympic Gold medalist Bobby Jones from Atlanta, US Open Champion Walter Hagan from Michigan, Jim Dowdy from Los Angeles, and famous trick-shot golfer Joe Kirkwood from New York, just to name a few. As a golfer, Tommy displayed his unique full-body swing in every state in the United States, every province in Canada, and every territory of Australia. He was also often captioned "America's foremost trick shot golf expert." As part of his indoor and outdoor exhibitions, Tommy would drive a ball from the crystal of a watch and then go himself one better by driving a ball off a human forehead or body part. In both instances he use only a Life Savers candy to separate the ball from the watch or forehead. Folks loved it! For the rehearsals of the golf act, my grandma worked as his assistant at first. At some point, Tommy drove a golf ball from some Life Savers resting on her forehead. Now, that's called true love! She had absolute confidence in his abilities. To his credit in using his wife, my dad (his son), or his grandkids as a golf tee, he never missed... ever. Doing so would have caused a concussion and contusions at a minimum. The only explanation for never having broken a watch crystal or skin on a forehead is his sheer power of concentration. This power has been a significant factor in producing measurable, repeatable results in both his life and his golf game.

Over the years, Tommy's game improved almost twenty strokes, and he attributed this improvement in large part to his mental discipline in the game. Whenever things went very well, and Tommy sank a putt or hit a good shot, he would sometimes do a little soft shoe tap dance. He was always fun to watch on the golf course. During his early days, it was sometimes a family affair, and Wally Fisher, his other grandson, was honored and proud to have the opportunity to caddie for him back in the 1950s. Unfortunately, I was too young and the bag too heavy. For the curious, his clubs were regulation; the length was forty-two and a half inches, the woods weighed sixteen ounces, and the irons fifteen ounces. He carried seventeen clubs, Bobby Jones 'Model 13' irons, and four off-the-rack drivers. Later in life, he had Jones adjust the heads of the clubs, allowing him to strike the ball more firmly. Believe it or not, he used every single club to a good advantage during a full eighteen holes. Tommy made club selection into part art and part science. Par was his best score, and he made par for eighteen holes four times during his life. Not bad for a guy with no arms or hands!

With a driver, Tommy's distance was about 150 to 200 yards. With irons, the yardage came in at about 100-125 yards. What he lacked in distance, he made up for in accuracy on the fairway. Tommy always hit straight golf balls! He attributed his ability to score so well to controlling his short game on the green and having a keen putting eye. According to OB Keller, who wrote for the Atlanta Journal newspaper for years and is considered by many to be at the time America's greatest golf writer, Tommy was considered a special golfer. Back in 1932, Keller wrote in his column: "Tommy McAuliffe is as much a genius with woods, irons, and putters as the renowned local Olympic Gold Metal Golfer Bobby Jones!" Tommy was deeply honored and later developed a fast friendship with the golfing great.

Known as the "Father of Professional Golf in America," Walter Hagen brought style, popularity, media, and big prize money to the sport in the 1920s and 1930s. Hagen is rated as one of the greatest golfers of all time, winning the US Open twice and the PGA Championship a record five times. He was also primarily responsible for Tommy and his family moving from upstate New York to Michigan and the opportunities of Motor City. In fact, he only played in one PGA event—the 1956 Motor City Open when in August of that year, he got to play with Arnold Palmer. It was the old school vs. the new school. Old pros like Hagen, Jones, Hogen, and Tommy were purposely stoic and reserved, while the new breed like Palmer, Kite, and Nicholas let it all hang out and showed emotions when making good or bad shots. The other animated discussion that took place with this tournament was the use of golf carts. Tommy hated them and would never use one, feeling that they were unnatural. Palmer withdrew the second round due to a hip problem. That allowed both of them to get to know each other, and Tommy enjoyed telling the old stories and showing Palmer around Tommy's new hometown. McAuliffe had a soft spot for Michigan since his days at Michigan State University and could smell opportunity. He loved the feel of Detroit. Besides, Tommy had always wanted to drive a car! •

69

Onstage Paramount Theater NYC 1928

CHAPTER 7
Dat's Showbiz

After the crash of 1929 and during the depression of the 1930s, America was looking for diversions and entertainment. Golf was in its golden age with big money, names and tournaments, and the theaters were full with the variety of vaudeville. It was the popular entertainment of the day. You could see a variety show for a dime with five or six different 'acts,' everything from singers, comedians, and jugglers to magicians and novelty acts like Tommy's. Beginning in the 1890s and through the 1930s, vaudeville was America's most popular form of entertainment. In its heyday, it had more than 1400 theaters and 25,000 performers. The continued growth of the lower-priced cinema in the early 1920s and the invention of 'Talkies,' motion pictures with sound, dealt the heaviest blow to vaudeville. By the start of WWII, it had faded into history.

McAuliffe did several exhibition golf tours across the country. In 1932, he had the pleasure of playing the Fox Theater in Detroit with his trick-shot golf show "Lucky 13". Being a hound for publicity and with the theater manager also doing his fair share, Tommy was put on the local radio station WJR, a 50,000 Watt giant AM Station with a signal that goes from northern Canada to the American Southland. When the hour for broadcasting arrived, he was not before the microphone and was nowhere to be found. After an intro as 'world champion armless golfer Tommy McAuliffe,' there was 60 seconds of awkward silence. Tommy finally got to the microphone, and in apologizing to the invisible radio audience, he humbly said,

"Gee, folks, really sorry I'm late. I was playing poker with the stage crew over at the beautiful Fox Theater, where I'll be appearing all next week. I'm not only late, but I lost my shirt, and oh boy, how I lost... You see, ladies and gentlemen, I didn't have any hands!"

The radio show host and station crew laughed for an hour.

After FDR's successful campaign for President in 1936, Tommy began to visit Congress in Washington DC more often in his efforts to get laws and programs passed that would help the handicapped. During one such visit, Tommy was getting shaved in one of the leading barbershops in town when a girl came over to his chair and asked if he wanted a manicure. Tommy was completely covered with the barber's cloth, and she did not notice his empty coat sleeves. Once realizing the predicament and after a bit of awkward silence, everyone in the barbershop burst out laughing. Tommy always believed that it is vital to keep a sense of humor about things. "Generally speaking, folks are too prone to showering sympathy upon individuals who, through circumstances, have lost their sight, become deaf, or even lost both arms as I have. I have always hated it," he related. "Just because a man has lost physical abilities, he is really no different as a person than any other individual. Besides, sympathy simply makes the giver feel better, not the receiver." But McAuliffe endured many a sympathetic comment during his life and would do so again as he met the public as an entertainer after his shows and exhibitions.

When the sound of bursting shells of WWI on the battlefields of Europe had faded, and the ammunition factories had ceased production across America, Tommy, like thousands of others, suddenly found himself out of a job. Again. Following the McAuliffe trail of '13' coincidences, he became unemployed on February 13, 1919. Tommy did not relish this unavoidable layoff because on January 13, just a month before, he "had made my life complete when Margaret Elizabeth O'Toole of Tacoma Washington agreed to become my wife." They had met and courted in college. In the ensuing years, she became much more than that and became his life counselor, intellectual equal, and financial partner. Tommy would always say that he owed much to the charming lady from the Pacific Northwest who, through the years, had proven to be the ideal wife and mother. But with three daughters and a son, a man can't be out of work long. Mrs. McAuliffe, my grandmother, took it all in stride. With a family to support, he had to find a source of income and right quick.

One day Tommy had a crazy notion, and with a friend as a partner, he entered the retail and wholesale coal and ice business. With a combined capital of $500, he purchased a rundown firm delivering these commodities to homes and businesses. He figured they were two necessities most folks had to have, so it would be a good investment. Aside from the government certificate to do business, the only 'asset' he had purchased was a sickly eight-year-old horse and a broken-down western wagon. Tommy and his partner were ambitious, and through diligent effort, the business survived. In 1925 the partnership was dissolved, and Tommy became the company.

Things went along pretty well until late 1928, the year before the big crash. 'McAuliffe Coal & Ice' was too liberal with credit to its customers, and one morning Tommy awakened to find that several of his clients had gone bankrupt. The due bills completely encompassed the firm's assets, and there was but one thing to do... close the office door. So he sadly did just that. It was another tough punch on the extended chin, but he said nothing. Tommy took the bitter medicine with a smile. Like most Americans in 1929, he was down but not out. Tommy's tough mental outlook had prepared him well for what was about to occur. From breadlines to bullets, he was ready for the future.

Times were tough. Suddenly, fifteen million Americans were out of a job, and wages were reduced 50-60 percent overnight. For the next six to ten years, it would be bread lines, haircuts at home, no beef, cabbage soup, and burlap cloth dresses. Being idle was no joke. Tommy needed income, and things were desperate, but naturally, like him, Tommy's wife again took the hit with a smile. She wanted to look for a job, but Tommy being of the old school, would not encourage it. It was her faith in him, her daily words of encouragement, which kept him moving forward and going from office to office and factory to factory, he would later share. Something had to be done and done quickly. And through it all, as a soothing source of comfort and clarity was the timeless game of Golf.

So necessity was the fact that inaugurated Golfer Tommy McAuliffe's entry into an active show business career. Self-preservation and a decent living for his four children and their lovable mother was the necessity that instituted the invention of the 'Lucky 13 Trick Shot Golf Show'. Forced to close the Coal and Ice company and unable to induce anyone to give him a 'real' job, the young father of four was faced with a pair of alternatives... One, he could accept charity and stay at home, or two, he could take his golf clubs into Vaudeville and show Business and be away from his home and loved ones. It was an easy decision to make. Charity was a non-starter, and while he did not relish leaving his growing family, he felt he simply had no choice. After much thought and prayer, he decided to try his luck being on stage in the crazy business of show. Golf was one of the fastest-growing sports in America at the time, but Golf clubs in Vaudeville? On a stage!? This idea seemed like a long shot. Tommy's little brother deserves the credit or blame. Walter had been doing amateur parts in theater and a short comedy 'show' at bars and gatherings around New York City. The skit was of such a nature that it could easily be modified to fit a golf act. The McAuliffe brothers lost no time in doing this, and within a week, they were deep into rehearsals.

"So there we were with an idea, one old golf club (yes, that one) and no modern stage experience. Gee, what could go wrong?" he laughed.

Tommy practiced day and night. One drill was chipping thirteen balls into a bushel basket at various locations in the family parlor over and over. Practice was required because it had been a few years since he had actually swung a club consistently. He was too busy earning a living. After a bit of practice, the old swing returned. Naturally, Tommy was happy. Happy because he had found his swing again and happy that he could possibly make a living again, but still, he was carrying a heavy heart over leaving his young family home alone. All of this happened between Christmas of 1927 and early 1928, which just goes to show how quickly things can fall into place if you let them, he would remember so many years later. "By '29, guys downtown were jumping out of ninth-floor windows because they had seemingly lost everything, so I considered myself very lucky," he said. He would always tell me the story of one of his friends in Buffalo who was swindled in the stock market, couldn't take the shame, and killed himself by jumping out of his office window. Tommy thought it was the ultimate waste, and he was angry that his friend had not contacted him for help. There were millions of stories like that after the crash, and some folks went back to wearing black arm-bands of WW I to indicate they had lost someone.

"So there we were, my brother and I, a single old golf club, a script for the act and the big bright idea that we would be a big hit on stage. And not just any stage but one only a block away from 'The Great White Way' of Broadway. Twice we put off our departure for New York City. For one thing, we were rather timid (hell, we were scared!), and second, we were both very poor. All right, have it your way—we were broke!" he confided. "But nothing ventured, nothing gained, and somehow we scraped together the train fare, and off we went." Once in the 'Big Apple' (it was called that even back then), they spent the next week going from theater to theater to try and get a paying gig. It was grueling work.

"Please, Sir, just a moment... I'm an armless golfer!" Tommy said urgently. The booker stopped and retraced his steps, his face full of seriousness now.

"Are you fellas trying to jive me?" he said suspiciously. "I play golf, and it's damn tough enough trying to hit that goddamn ball with two good arms, let alone with none. It can't be done without arms!" he stated as fact.

Tommy assured him that he was deadly serious and would gladly demonstrate to him as well as his entire staff. Tommy and his brother were ushered into the booker's small private office for the integration.

In an instant, Tommy's coat was off, and with a few golf balls, the old club, and a metal wastebasket, he went to work. He wound continually bounced the ball on the head of a club while he was talking. He lost no time chipping twelve out of a possible thirteen into the basket from one side of the office to the other. All the while telling jokes and a little bit about his positive thinking philosophy in a fun rapid staccato type delivery... After all, this was show business!

Observing a diploma on the wall, Tommy found that the man he just performed for was Jack Dempsey—not the fighter but one of the greatest unknown Broadway producers who ever lived. He gave the more famous Ziegfeld Follies a run for the money on Broadway for years. Tommy related as quickly as possible about how entertaining the act was and what he could do with a set of golf clubs (skipping the detail that at the time, he only had one club). He was relieved and encouraged now because Dempsey's interest seemed not to be passive as they puffed away at their cigarettes, which he had kindly provided. Tommy assured him that he was the only armless golfer in the world (something that was, in fact, unknown) and also told him that he and Walter knew how to do promotion and put butts in the seats, which of course was music to the booker's ears.

"After a while, there was a pause in the conversation, and then, "So how would you like to go down to West Point on Sunday as one of my acts to entertain the graduating Army cadets?" he asked matter of factly.

"Gladly, gladly, gladly!" we said, our chests puffing out. And so we got our first gig.

"As we confidently strolled back to the good old Somerset Hotel on 47th Street, where many performers stayed, we felt we had made a new friend in booker Jack Dempsey, and we couldn't have been happier. Sunday arrived, and we went down to West Point and did our little act, which went over very well with the Army cadets. We talked about the art of golf and the art of living. It went well, and things were looking up," Tommy

said as he sipped his favorite drink: a highball Gin
and Tonic with a wedge of lime.

He was always all about planning and rehearsal.
Tommy felt that planning and rehearsal were
critical to success, whether it was an act for the
stage or eighteen holes of golf. Folks will tell you,
for example, that when they played golf with him,
he was always thinking and planning two or three
strokes ahead. (He would later tell me that it was
two or three holes ahead, not strokes!) Pre-
planning and repetitive action towards perfection
was another life rule he would often repeat to me.

But like many, he found show business to be less
than glamorous. While he was waiting to sign on
to a full tour, Tommy had played several gigs in
and around New York City, but like everyone in
entertainment, his bookings were hard hit by the
depression. His ever-faithful agent Patty Schwartz
promised Tommy bookings every day, but they
always somehow failed to materialize. Before long,
together with his traveling partner, they found
themselves alone, hungry, and broke. It was hard
to keep a smile going when one's stomach was in
pain.

They had not eaten in four days. One evening,
they were sitting in their room in the Somerset
Hotel when a fellow performer came in. He was a
popular singer. (I believe this to be Tony Bennett
but could not confirm it; however, Grandpa talked

about Mr. Benedetto, Tony Bennett's real name.-ED) Looking them straight in the eyes, Tony said:

"Let's go have supper!"

"Just had it," they said.

"Where and what did you have?" Tony shot back.

"Chicken pie at the little coffee shop up the street," the two asserted.

"Oh, well, then you can join me for dessert," offered Tony.

"No thanks, Tony, we will stay here and read," they responded.

"Sure you don't want something to eat?" He came back to them as he took a step near the door.

"No, we're filled, thanks," was the assurance. The truth was that the mere mention of food made their tummies do all sorts of somersaults. They were hungry. Their spritely answers must've betrayed their true selves because with fire in his eyes, their guest Tony came closer and his Italian eyes opening wide as he literally shouted:

"You're a pair of damn good Irish liars! You haven't eaten in four damn days... Why didn't you tell me you were broke? Here's $10, and when that's gone, there's more," he said matter of factly.

The two were speechless and simply stared at each other for what seemed like ten minutes. They admitted they were starving. Off to the Cafe where the performers did more than justice to their first meal in four days, so much so, the waitress had to put in for overtime!

As they walked back to the hotel, Tony remarked:

"Don't you fellas know that show business people stick together and help each other? All you got to do is ask!" (But Grandpa would always say that asking for help is the hard part for some people.) Tony was a giver like most all showbiz folks, and he was also right about something else—it was Tommy's personal pride that prevented him from asking for help.

Matters went along swimmingly until the fall of 1930, a result of the '29 crash, no doubt. Then like a brick wall, the bottom fell out of show business. Folks simply could not afford a show at the local theater anymore, even if it was 'only ten cents.' The new thing called movies was also changing the way people were entertained.

Tommy's agents in Chicago, LA, and New York City could not secure any significant bookings. Days, weeks, and months went by, and he still took it all in stride, always keeping a smile on his face. There were a few golf exhibitions here and there, but the pay was insignificant compared to being paid on a tour. Meanwhile, almost daily letters from his agents told him they were trying, and they would have something in a week or two. McAuliffe's other daily mail consisted of bills, bills, and more bills from merchants who had been very

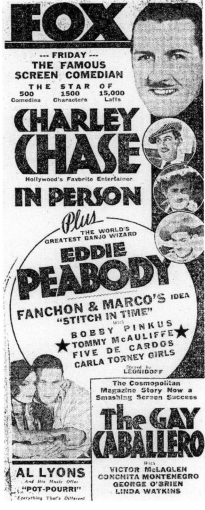

kind in extending him credit. "I had no money, and again I was out of work," he remembered. "We had put every cent into over living and into the house, but sadly and shortsightedly, I had kept nothing significant for reserves. I consider myself fairly smart, but that was a huge mistake," he said. "Always pay yourself first," and I always have.

Tommy's outlook was not the best during this time because of the overdue bills and the high-pressure debt collectors calling all the time and some even coming by the house. Having a positive mindset is vital in one's rehabilitation, in the game of golf, and in being a good entertainer. "I was not in the best of moods due to the situation. Then came a notice from the bank that they must have the money, actually, only six months of interest, or they would foreclose on our home," he said. "At least they didn't want an arm and a leg!"

Tommy's back was to the wall in every respect. It was now the fall of 1932. All in all, it was not a happy outlook that confronted him... again. It would've been easy to just give up, throw in the towel, and call it a day. But showbiz folks, golfers, and guys named McAuliffe are troopers, not quitters. His family lived an hourly prayer that agents would somehow come through with bookings or there would be another way to gain income.

"Some gigs came, but not enough, and the thought of losing our home and its furnishings was also eating my darling wife's heart out," he said. "We were in trouble, and I was frantic because I was truly helpless to do anything to prevent the promised foreclosures." It was a valuable lesson he would relay to his young grandson many years later. The feeling of helplessness and lack of control over one's life, real or imagined, can be one of the most disabling things that a person can ever face. But somehow, Tommy overcame that too. Over the years, I was made to understand (as he sat me on top of his big wooden desk time after time) that to him, being controlled by others was the ultimate indignity.

He was a good Catholic man, and on the 13th day of a solemn religious novena the McAuliffe family was making, God suddenly answered their prayers. Naturally and strangely, it was on August 13th, just two weeks before the deadline, when Tommy received a wire from Los Angeles offering him a full vaudeville tour with the famous 'Frenchon & Marco variety show.' "I was overcome with joy, and so were all my creditors! Now I could save our home and have something to bank on... At least for now. So, onward I went into the glittering and cutthroat world of show business. My contract with the show production company had been signed, and although I was not scheduled to go to work until February, I was guaranteed thirty-two weeks of work," he explained.

Tommy's family settled into a six-room furnished flat, and he set out for the West Coast to fulfill his show business contract leaving New York on January 13, 1933, by train. Due to his financial circumstances and the state of the economy, he accepted the tour at a little more than half his regular show fee. The tour required forty-two exhausting weeks of second class travel, mostly by train, to play thirty-two shows. It went very well, and Tommy arrived home to his family just before Christmas 1932 with a small profit from the tour. In the following years, there were other tours. But for all the glamour, the newspaper and magazine articles, the radio interviews, and the theater appearances—not to mention the time away from his precious family—he would say, shaking his head: "Don't tell me that show business is easy."

"My homestay was not for long because my agents promised to have additional work for me within a couple of weeks. I was very pleased because I wanted to be with my family for the Christmas holidays. As 1933 passed into history, I was still idle, and other than a few appearances and exhibitions, that was pretty much the end of Vaudeville and my show business career."

Grandpa would always say that one of the most enjoyable facets of his pseudo-celebrity and the novelty of being a 'world champion armless golfer' was the doors it would open and being able to visit hospitals and rehabilitation centers for both veterans and children. He would simply stop by to talk, listen, and joke with the patients, leaving them with his 'No Handicaps' message.

"One of the most enjoyable visits I have ever experienced was at the home for crippled children in Pittsburgh, Pennsylvania. Several days after that unforgettable visit, I received a total of sixty-seven letters from patients there (the hospital specializes in children that have lost a limb)," he explained. "The following letter from that group is typical of the thousands I received in my travels across America. Its simplicity and sincerity stamp it as a real gem, and things like this are worth 100 standing ovations to me."

"Dear Mr. McAuliffe,
    Just wanted to drop a line to say thanks for your visit the other day. We had a very enjoyable and interesting time seeing all the things that you've accomplished even with your handicap. I always try to look at mine in the same way and that word "smile "is the big thing. You certainly did bring a lot of cheer to us and I know that can't will never enter my mind or vocabulary again. Wishing you the best of luck and happiness. Oh yes, and please don't forget the picture! Thanks
Your new friend,
David Lloyd
PS: Sir, have you ever hit a Sandtrap?"

"I can still see his fourteen-year-old beaming face as he sat next to me on the spacious green lawn in the back of their wonderful facility, and I can still see his grin as soon as I chipped golf balls into a bushel basket as we ate peanut butter and jelly sandwiches with him and his pals. I responded:

"Dear David,
Of course I've hit Sandtrap's, both on the golf course and in life! The biggest one I ever hit was when I lost both my arms. But I got out of the sand trap by taking my wedge called "mental guts" and blasted out of the Sandtrap, and here I am out on the fairway of life hitting the ball hard, often and straight so that eventually it will hit the green and that little ball will go into the round cup. Keep your eye on the target of success in your life. Please remember what I told you the other day, that there is no handicap in life except a mental one!
Your sincere pal,
Tommy McAuliffe"

Tons of wonderful things have been written and said about Tommy over the years. But he would always say that while he fully appreciated all of them, he often felt the compliments were not always fully deserved. For example, writing in the New York Times in 1938 long-time columnist William Smith wrote:

"The career of world-famous armless golfer Tommy McAuliffe should be an inspiration to every youth in our country. What boy ever entered upon a life with such a disadvantage. Tommy overcame all his obstacles with a grin and a will to overcome. Good looking, clean-cut, and to all other appearances, a normal young man. He also makes an excellent public speech. He has a personality that breeds confidence. That ever-present smile wins the hearts of those who meet him. There is no man today who deserves the credit due Tommy McAuliffe. He alone won his fight. The loss of his two arms at the age of nine was not the biggest problem; it was the mental feeling of helplessness that is sure to permeate one's mind under such unfortunate conditions. Winning that battle takes perseverance. The compliment of every person in our country should go to him. He may well be put on a pedestal as a model to American youth. Tommy McAuliffe is a man's man."

Tommy would always take such kudos with a grain of salt and would always say, "It's nice to be important, but it's more important to be nice!"

This author was bitten with the show business bug early in life as a wanna-be singer and comedian, and I would ask him for advice and about what it was like entertaining thousands. I remember him always saying that entertaining people was one of the greatest rewards of his life and that humor and being able to make people laugh is one of God's greatest and most special gifts. Tommy was able to both entertain with his golf tricks and reach folks' hearts with his story of overcoming and making the most of life with God's gifts.

The end of the 1930s did not see the end of his show biz endeavors but rather a morphing into public advocacy for the handicapped and speaking engagements about positive thinking and his 'No Handicaps' philosophy. He would use his infirmities and good humor to gain access to the influential and powerful. •

CHAPTER 8
Halls of Power

Ever since he was a lad, Tommy thought about someday being elected to public office. He deeply loved and believed in America. In 1926, he tried to realize this ambition by seeking election as a New York State Senator. With no campaign funds or political experience, naturally, he was defeated, but he was not disgraced. He brought up some important issues in the campaign: equal and fair treatment under the law and opportunities for the disabled. The discussion of these issues was sorely needed, and they were, for the most part, not being discussed. Defeats were nothing new to Tommy, and he learned that while he liked public service, the rough and tumble world of politics was not for him. When his opponent inferred that somehow because of having no arms, he was less than a man and that the Irish were less than honorable people, McAuliffe almost withdrew from the race. He also hated asking voters for campaign donations.

"I'm interested in helping people find new courage, be renewed, and then be successful in playing the game of life. Through Golf, I have both entertained people and learned lifelong lessons on how to live a fulfilling life and be a better citizen," he said during one campaign speech. "Many of the disabled and Veterans, in particular, are disconnected from the workforce, have little access to significant social and cultural information, and have limited opportunities to participate in community life. We need to change that!" he would say from the stump.

Golf and Tommy's unique abilities were a calling card and provided entry into the halls of power. Captains of industry that wouldn't give an appointment suddenly would. Senators and congressmen who would not give a lobbyist the time of day would gladly give Tommy time to talk Golf, and if his issues came up... well, that certainly would not stop the round. Wisely, he would save the heavy stuff until the back nine!

With the entry of our great country into WWII the the Curtis Airplane Company went into increased production. "I knew several of my pals were employed by Curtis, and it was a powerful up-and-coming company. They suggested that I call upon the employment manager and make an application. After deciding my course of action, I called the airplane employment office. I got in without trouble and was asked to be seated with others waiting to be seen," Tommy said. "Each was seen, as were many others who came in after me. I resented such treatment. Over an hour lapsed, and still, I sat. When I could stand it no longer, I asked if I was to receive some consideration."

"I'll be with you in just a moment," replied the employment manager.

After writing a few more memos and caring for three more men who came in after I had, the employment chief turned to me and said:

"What can I do for you, young man?"

"I want to work!" was my rapid reply.

He looked at me in astonishment. Honestly, he actually just stared at me for a few moments. I sensed he must've thought that I called for a handout or something like that. I held my ground despite the silence. Finally, I ventured a question:

"Is there anything strange about me asking for work?" The question was never answered.

After a deadly silence, this remark pierced my ears; "I don't know what I could give you that you could do and we could get away with it."

"Sir!" I almost shouted, "I don't want to get away with anything. I came here to secure work, and I am fully capable of doing just that. If you haven't anything for me, I will appreciate you giving me a pass into the factory to see Mr. Norman Benton and Mr. James Barthel; they are friends of mine." Without further ado, I got the pass and was dismissed."

Tommy continued, "My pal Jimmy took me in tow, and I was taken to the production manager's office. After questioning me for fifteen minutes, I

US Capitol Indoor Putting Green 1938

was assigned as Production Chief in Charge of Factory and Allied Government Inspections! The production manager did not insult my intelligence, nor did he figure a man without arms was helpless. He simply asked me questions. He was looking for men with gray matter and frankly told me so. He boldly told me he thought I was the man he was looking for. And I will always be grateful to him as it took courage for him to choose someone out of the normal."

McAuliffe believed the inroads the handicapped need to make are not just in Washington DC but also in the offices of corporate America. Relating the incident with the employment manager was simply to show that he was no different than thousands of other managers who actually think that the physically challenged are helpless individuals looking for a handout. "They forget that it was brains and their proper use which made them a success and not the fact that they carried two arms and legs. It seems to me an asset can evolve from the Depression and from the War. With the physically handicapped and the thousands of war vets to come, our country needs to open its heart and mind to this sector of our citizenry and use it for the productive resource it is," Tommy said. "Every citizen, every employer, every new business owner should agree that there should be fair wages and opportunity for all, in spite of any real or perceived handicap. We should make this the law of the land, and we will."

Once content with the opportunity to simply give people food for thought in solving public problems, McAuliffe also saw the government bureaucracy and the uneven playing field handicapped people faced under the law first hand. He became determined to change it for the better or at least bring handicapped rights to the forefront of the day's political discussion. His quick humor and skill with a golf club, despite his affliction, provided entry not only to show business folk and high society but also to politicians and officials at the state capitol and inside Congress in Washington DC. Basically, anyone who played golf was a fan and was willing to speak with him. Officeholders would call him a natural-born lobbyist and he was.

The late 1930s and early '40s saw Tommy spending more and more time in Washington DC. One interesting match Tommy had was with Senator Royal Copeland, D, New York (1923-1938). During the round, they talked about rehabilitation, the great need for returning WWII vets to have access to these vital services, and how equality for all under the law should be our national goal. By the end of the eighteen holes, the good Senator was a fan (see letter).

"I was honored to be invited to Capitol Hill several times to testify before Congress and assist in getting action on rehabilitation bills in the Senate and House of Representatives. We got it done, and these bills enabled various states to fund the needed work of human rehabilitation, which was especially important to the many returning World War II vets," Tommy related.

"More needed to be done, so it was arranged that I could do a little demonstration for those in Congress on the steps of the Capitol. I was thrilled, and on a sunny day in May, I showed them what could be done with a golf club despite physical imperfections. While doing so, I talked about the necessity of passing legislation so that the handicapped might be aided through education and training to be useful and productive citizens of our great nation. It went over quite well, and the measures soon passed with bipartisan support!"

Tommy spent most of the late 1940s and '50s giving positive thinking talks and speeches to groups throughout the country. He only had two requirements during such engagements: one, there was to be no inference of sympathy during his introduction... no "The poor man..." or "It's a shame he has no arms..." etc. and two, there must always be a fresh glass of water covered by a clean white handkerchief on the table or podium. And there always was. In the early 1960s, after a successful career in the life insurance business (he became a lifetime member of the salesman's 'Million Dollar Roundtable'), he established 'McAuliffe Insurance Repair Co.,' a home repair business that my dad worked part-time at while also being a full-time Detroit Fire Fighter. Robert,

Tommy's son, drove the back of the long hook and ladder fire truck—one of the most dangerous driving positions.

Tommy McAuliffe was also involved with the passage of various rehabilitation-related laws and measures which gave handicapped citizens equal protection and opportunity under the laws and regulations of the United States. These included the Social Security Act of 1935 (he was a big supporter of President Roosevelt and was a full-time volunteer for FDR and the Democratic Party during the 1936 campaign). Other measures included the 1943 and 1954 Vocational Rehab Amendments, which laid the groundwork for the 1965 Vocational Rehabilitation Act. Two years before his death and after his passing, his testimony helped pass the groundbreaking Rehab Act of 1973. Tommy must have been smiling down from heaven on that day.

Because of his activities in the field of rehabilitation during the early 1940s, McAuliffe was also considered to be selected as head of the Federal Rehabilitation Bureau and to be put in charge of all federal policy related to handicap programs and services. He withdrew from consideration for the post because it would have meant moving to Washington DC, which he was unwilling to do. Being politically involved was important to him. He used to tell me that if a man didn't vote, he had no right to complain. He was right. •

CHAPTER 9
No Handicaps

As I looked through Grandpa Tommy's old typewritten papers with notes in the margins, it was clear to me that Tommy's real purpose was to show that nothing is impossible with the proper mindset and effort. His follow-through was that the principles learned in the crazy game of golf can help both the physically perfect as well as the imperfect to achieve the most out of life, regardless of station or physical condition. "My goal is to spread the gospel that 'there is no handicap in life except a mental one.'"

It was suddenly 1952, and the McAuliffe family was very happy with their new home in Motor City. I recall that his modest three-bedroom, two-bath ranch home in Southwest Detroit had grey siding with white aluminum awnings over the major windows. It had a separate garage (Tommy had always wanted to drive a car! He talked about self-driving cars, push-button phones, and voice automation which would not be invented for another fifty years!) and a large backyard for BBQs.

Tommy loved Motown and was a big Detroit Tigers fan; he loved Lafayette Coney Island hot dogs, Stroh's beer, Vernor's ginger ale, and Sanders candies. All made in Detroit. A regular event was a fancy dinner out at McGuire's restaurant where the three McAuliffe girls would get up and sing. The home on Kentfield Avenue was modest, and the large dutch Elm trees lining the street provided ample shade in the summer. In the winter, when the snow stuck to the trees, it made the street a winter wonderland tunnel. And Tommy would always sweep or shovel his own walkway. Self-reliance was one of the things he insisted upon. Recalling my visits to his home, I remember that all the furniture, which we kids were not allowed to sit on, was covered with clear heavy-duty plastic. Heck, we were not even allowed in the living room. I was told that it was for guests, and being the smart ass I was, I once said, "Then, what am I?" I got no ice cream on that visit. The carpet pathways also had plastic protection runners, and my grandma kept the home as clean as a hospital.

Tommy's friend, golf legend Walter Hagen, who lived up north in Traverse City, Michigan, had encouraged him to move due to a booming economy and all the opportunities there with the auto industry. Besides, Tommy always had a soft spot for Michigan from his time at college. "We were getting a big kick out of our new car, and I was writing down ideas for an invention that would allow me to drive. We were truly enjoying life again after our past setbacks," he said. All this happiness came as a result of Tommy's vaudeville tours, which were a roaring success and proved lucrative. He felt good that hard work and a few breaks could lead to achieving the American dream... the fact he had no arms was not—and he felt should not be—a factor. "All we're looking for is an equal opportunity and fair treatment under the law," he would always say.

On February 13, 1933, the Director of Rehabilitation in the state of New York called to tell Tommy he had located him a job with the County. He went to work that day at $17 a week, which was raised to $20 a week that August. Tommy was made Assistant Executive Director in charge of the Investigations Department. Things were looking up. The increased earnings made it possible to purchase much-needed clothing for the wife and kids. When the Federal Civil Works Administration (CWA) came into existence, Tommy was directly involved and received more money per week. "During the life of our local CWA, I handled nearly $2 million of federal funding... not bad for a guy with no hands, eh?" When an audit was performed the next year, it was found that Tommy was $.10 in the black. He was with CWA until 1936, when the Republican party gained control of the program and its board. Shortly thereafter, he was removed for the insane reason that "he did not fit into the new executive director's vision of things," but it became known that it was really because of Tommy's work for the Democratic Party. These sorts of house cleanings were par for the course for government appointees. So Tommy was idle again with just another sock on the extended chin, and "a good reason to always vote!"

The storm clouds of war began to get darker as the day of infamy, December 7, 1941, lay at Tommy's doorstep, and some more hits would be forthcoming both for him and for America. "Hard knocks form a vital part of life. They make us better and stronger and should not be avoided," he'd say. "Show me somebody who has had it easy in life, and usually, I'll show you somebody with no character." It had been a rough road so far, but the challenges that lay ahead appeared to be insurmountable. But Tommy, like all Americans, was ready to roll up his sleeves and get to work to win the war and save freedom for the world.

"My hope has always convinced me that the best for me lies ahead, but Christmas 1941 found that very hard to believe in. Faith is also like a vision, and without that vision, my life would've been an empty one. Without a full dose of faith, I would not have been able to prove the 'No Handicaps' philosophy," he asserted. "To live life fully, every individual, regardless of race, creed, physical makeup, or condition, must have a full measure of enduring hope and faith. The funny thing was that being out of a job only increased my supply of hope, and with that hope, I had faith in myself to go out and do the proper things that would lead me to success," he said. Tommy would have never reached the green if he didn't tee off, and he taught me that there are many people in this life who are simply afraid of failure so much so that they never put the ball on the tee.

To help illustrate the point about mind over matter, Grandpa would always share and tell the story about a visit he made to talk with returning war troops at a large Army base hospital at the end of WWII. During the visit, he met a young sergeant of the United States Army who called him aside and told him the following story... It seems that a member of his outfit, the 101st Airborne, had gotten stranded behind enemy lines on the Italian/German border. In trying to make his way back to his unit, he jumped on board a passing freight train, hopefully, headed in the right direction.

The boxcar looked brand new and had swastikas all over it, so he felt sure no one would look for him in there. As the various train cars hit bumps along the tracks, the train jostled, and the sliding door of his boxcar suddenly slammed shut and locked tight. At first, the soldier was relieved because he thought he would be secure within the boxcar from the enemy. However, slowly, he realized that the boxcar was one of the new refrigerated 'iceboxes on wheels' that the innovative German army was using to move meats, poultry, and produce to the troops in the southern regions of the German Reich. Refrigerated 'Reefer' cars first came on the scene in 1851 via Northern Railways in the US.

He began to panic. "Surely, I'm going to freeze to death and die in this damn boxcar," said the worried Corporal. He found a piece of coal on the car floor and began to write out his epitaph and a last message to his family. "Got separated from unit, gonna freeze to death, please tell family I love them very much."

By the morning, the Allies had liberated the destination of the train. As the train rolled into the station, the Allied troops opened up each car one by one... And sure enough, they found the American soldier frozen dead from hypothermia and exposure. However, later, upon examining the refrigeration unit of the train car, it was found to be defective, and due to the local weather, officials said that the car temperature never dropped below 40°, the young soldier explained to Tommy.

"It was simply the man's mind that killed him!" asserted Tommy. "So, when people tell me that one can't have control over one's mind and that thoughts are not that powerful, I say... bull!" Whether real or simply wartime urban legend, the story's point about the power of the human mind still rings true.

He once sat me down to talk about opportunities and how potential is fleeting. He would talk about the guy who for years sold him his suits. "For twenty years, John was my guy for suits. Just an ordinary courteous clothing salesman, he would ask his customers all sorts of questions and, after hours, would study the products his store offered. The years had taken their toll, and he was about to quit. Then one day, without warning, the head of the store passed away, and John suddenly became manager. Today, the same John is in charge of not just the entire store but the entire chain of stores. The lesson is he made good use of his opportunities for bettering himself every day, so when the opportunity came his way, he was ready for it," he said. "In golf, too, we see when a

Regulation golf clubs made for Tommy by Bobby Jones

good player will have a plan and set up his shots from Tee to Cup. How many times have we set off down the fairway of life, but the ball didn't roll quite our way? It's having skills needed when you hit the rough that brings you back onto the fairway, and that makes the difference between just a player and a true champion. Yes, the lesson is in the playing and the planning.

A champion uses all of his opportunities every day. In salesman John's case, knowing more about the customers he served and his stores' merchandise, he profited from his mistakes, and when the time arrived for the real test, he was ready because he was better equipped. Through his many errors and failures, he had built within himself a depth of knowledge and courage," Tommy asserted. "Just like when you're on the Golf Course doing those trick shots over and over or those eight-hour practice sessions... Those efforts will give you the skills you need when you hit the rough, and you're behind a big bush that's between you and the hole. Tom, you be ready when your time comes!" He said sincerely. I've always remembered that talk.

McAuliffe's philosophy of positive thinking, tough love, and sheer determination has proven helpful to all. My grandfather, Tommy McAuliffe, died in 1967 from Cancer and heart problems. In 2021, notes, press clippings, and a hand-done unpublished manuscript called 'No Handicaps' were found in an attic. First written between the years 1937 to 1939 but never published, it will be available in the near future via bookstores and online outlets. A positive thinking advocate long before it was popular, what I find most remarkable about the manuscript is not just the futuristic mind over matter philosophy, which was far ahead of its time, but also the fact that Tommy pounded out each and every letter, one by one on a manual typewriter with a pencil in his teeth. He could have given up when that streetcar took his arms and hands, but instead, he called a Mulligan!

So many years later, I remember seeing a big sign on his bathroom mirror one time that said, 'There is no handicap in life except a mental one!' I used to enjoy watching my grandmother shave him. "I have come to understand that there really are 'No Handicaps' except in one's mind," he would always profess. "I found these principles helpful with both my own rehabilitation and life as well as in the game of golf. I have found that playing golf requires not just physical strength but a strong mental game as well," he said. And when it comes to being in command of one's mental attitude, Tommy would know.

He was a positive influence in my life, and I always felt good about myself when I was around him or after a visit. His inspirational life story continues to be a beacon for all who hear it, and I consider myself one of the luckiest grandsons on the planet for having known... 'Mr. Mulligan'.

THE END

CHAPTER 10
Pictures & Clips

<u>A Cultivating Swing</u>

Such a clever lad. Quicker than a shadow. Oh his ability to put the small white ball in the little hole was par for all to see. All the gang said he's our honey and they backed him with their money. When the ball rolled not his way they couldn't seem to get him down to the wonder of the Butch. The other fellows knew it, they thought he couldn't do it. He grinned and thought life so fancy and found a swing calm and quiet. Let the fancy swingers run riot. He found the chance he needed and landed on the green and on the mat they're lying reposing, found a winning team. They held the man a winner, he's got a swing punch but there was nothing new about his story no it's just an allegory. There is a moral think it over, it's a tip and there are a bunch. Life's an 18 hole round and in case you want to do it and win it, cultivate your swing.

By Tommy McAuliffe
Poem written in 1936

The United States Senate
Washington, DC
Read into the Congressional Record

No one can hear Tom McAuliffe's story without taking a new look at life most of us think life is pretty tough especially these days we find a lot of fault because things are not passed to us on a silver platter sometimes. If that is our attitude his story should put us to shame! With half our equipment he has twice the courage and optimism of any average man.

Is it pure selfishness or cowardice that makes so many of us consider that we have handicaps in the game of life? Be it physical or mentally? Why do we limit ourselves when a man without arms says "I have no handicaps!" This man overcame obstacles which would drive many a weak soul to suicide. Instead of morning and lamenting and wailing and worrying Tommy looked at life square in the face and brushed aside every natural instinct to loaf the rest of his days. His is the stuff of which legends are made.

What McAuliffe did should be an inspiration to every limited person in all the world. It should renew the enthusiasm of those who are striving for rehabilitation or just trying to live their best life. It's an outstanding example of what willpower can do.

World famous Blind, Deaf and Mute Helen Keller, who learned to communicate with the no assets and World Champion Armless Golfer Tommy McAuliffe are the King and Queen in the royal family of spunk! Their splendid achievements are an inspiration and we shall never cease to pay homage to their majestic bravery.

If I had my way I should make Tommy McAuliffe a wandering evangelist traveling from institution to institution where cripple persons of the body or mind are found. But first we need to get him off the golf course! I would endow him so that he could spend the rest of his life seeking out and encouraging men and women who have suffered similar accidents. His example and courage will inspire others to go and do likewise.

My hat is off to World Champion Armless Golfer Tommy McAuliffe!

Senator Royal S. Copeland
United States Senate D-NY
Chairman, Subcommittee on the Handicapped
1937

Let it be known...

That Tommy McAuliffe is 'the Rehab Man'! "I will succeed!
" that's what you always say and do. Your 'No Handicaps'
philosophy has and will help millions of disabled Veterans
and the handicapped. You've always assumed you could
succeed and you always say you will succeed not if I
succeed, there are no 'maybes'. You've been met with
many difficulties throughout life but you always meet them
head on... you size up the challenge, plan your drive down
the fairway and then follow through to the hole.

One of your fellow newsmen in Washington DC I think
summed it up beautifully during his recent news column;
"Tommy McAuliffe carries the empty coat sleeves tucked
in the pockets of his coat... Not as a badge of defeat, but
rather as an emblem of distinction." You have faith in
yourself which is evident when you talk. You come from
conviction with faith in yourself and the you are at par
with any other person or group. You ask and accept no
service that you can perform yourself. Your actions are an
evidence of "no handicaps" because believing you have
none you ask for no special favor; Not in business and not
on the Golf Course. You always set

high standards for yourself even with the presence of a
physical disability great enough to render many a person

utterly helpless. There's no excuse in your mind and there is no self-pity, self-consciousness or malingering in your make up.

The factors that have made your life a success and a reality are well expressed by writer Charles Dickens when he said "think hard, work constantly and make the best of things as they come along with a good or bad result resolutely determined not to be discouraged."

The self-realized methods you've learned to utilize have effected your success and have proven to be the backbone of any great rehabilitation plan. Professional or amateur these life tools may be used to advantage by both the physically disabled and the physically normal. Indeed I believe you have indeed created a new type of man, 'the rehab man', the rehabilitation man is a new man that despite any physical infirmity refuses to be 'less than' and won't take no for an answer. Those invisible arms you carry in your head you have learned to use well. You, Tommy McAuliffe, are an inspiration and a man to be respected in life, the Boardroom and Golf Course.

Gov. Frank Murphy
Michigan - D
1938 (Governor's Proclamation)

Big Food Show

TOMMY M'AULIFFE

The picture shows Tommy McAuliffe, armless golfer, who will entertain at Tiedtke's food show this week. Tommy can operate a typewriter with a pencil held between his teeth.

WHAT was surely the strangest golf match ever played was staged at Dorchester, Mass., recently, when Joe Sweeney, Boston's famous one-armed golfer, played a round with Tom McAuliffe, Buffalo's armless player. A large gallery followed the unique match and enthusiastically cheered the courage of the sportsmen who have surmounted unusual handicaps. McAuliffe won, 94 to 96, medal play.

BOSTON EVENING AMERICAN WEDNESDAY, APRIL 20, 193—

NO ARM VS. 1 ARM AT GOLF

JOSEPH SWEENEY   TOM McAULIFFE

The strangest golf match ever beheld—a sight that would have gladdened the hearts of the Geneva disarmament conference—was witnessed on the Franklin Park links today when Joseph Sweeney, Boston's famous one-armed golfer, played Tom McAuliffe, the no-armed golf marvel, who is showing audiences at the Metropolitan this week how he plays without hands. A

Big Food Show

A food show was opened by Tiedtke's Monday. It will continue through Saturday.

Food manufacturers throughout the country, who are co-operating with Tiedtke's in conducting the show, have informed store officials that this show will be the largest to be held in any store between New York and Chicago.

Orange growers from California, several flour manufacturers, meat packers, cereal manufacturers, candy makers and others will have experts at the show for demonstration purposes, officials of the store said Monday. An oriental tea booth will be a feature. Souvenirs will be distributed.

Tommy McAuliffe, armless golfer on the Paramount bill this week, will be an added attraction for the food show. He will provide entertainment on Tiedtke's third floor Tuesday, Wednesday and Thursday. McAuliffe can make difficult shots at golf and can operate a typewriter with a pencil held between his teeth.

comedy and novelty, with Tommy McAuliffe, an armless trick golf wizard furnishing many surprises. Earl Le Vere and Mildred Bryan in an eccentric comedy turn, win most of the laughs on the bill.

DETROIT FREE PRESS

Dancing, singing, acrobatics and skill in several directions feature the Fanchon and Marco idea "Stitch in Time," with Tommy McAuliffe, the armless golfer, to enthuse devotees of the game with his deftness. There is some delightful dancing by the Carla Torney girls and stepping of a different type by Benda Torso. Earl Lavere and Mildred Bryant in comedy patter; Harriet Mortimer, with songs, and the tumbling and juggling of the Five DeCardos, offer a diversity of talent. Popular torch songs are woven into an orchestra overture with Steve Weninger as soloist.

Loss of Arms No Handicap To McAuliffe

Armless Golf Wonder in Exhibition at Glenwood Links

IN golf handicaps are something to be overcome. In life, handicaps must be treated in much the same manner. At least Tommy McAuliffe, a young man who comes to the Glenwood golf club Thursday afternoon for an exhibition match, says so. Tommy overcame both physical and golf handicaps and is the only man in the world who plays golf, and good golf, without the use of his arms. The reason for this is that both arms are off at the shoulders.

Tommy, not yet 20 years old, was but nine when a railroad train amputated both arms. In the years that followed he has successfully overcome all the obstacles and handicaps that have faced him both on the golf course and in everyday life.

A great game of golf is just the ordinary thing in Tommy's life. He drives 150 yards on an average. He was for 13 years a sports writer on a newspaper, and never missed an edition. Minus his arms, Tommy can write his name or any other words as legibly as anyone.

He says he has the advantage over most golfers inasmuch as he never has to worry over whether or not he is using his wrists properly, or wonder about which grip is the best, or fret about his follow through. McAuliffe has one grip and it always works. He breaks 90 on almost any course, no matter how difficult.

Tommy demonstrates far better than anyone can describe on paper. He is in reality a sort of phenomenon. His clubs are of regulation make and are equipped with no special apparatus to simplify holding. He uses no tricks, although his grip is necessarily a little different than that of the ordinary golfer. Tommy teaches a lesson in perseverance as well as expert and trick golfing.

Tickets for the match will be on sale at the local golf clubs as well as downtown agencies, to be announced later.

Trick Golfer

Tommy McAuliffe, who is seen in "Stitch in Time" at the Imperial Theatre. One of America's trick golfers, he plays without arms, striking the ball by holding his club between his neck and shoulders.

UNUSUAL MATCH AT HARTFORD GOLF

One of the strangest matches ever played on local fairways will get going Tuesday morning at the Hartford Golf club when Tommy McAuliffe, who lost both his arms in an accident, will nevertheless carry off his part in a foursome. Tommy swings clubs by his teeth—and, what is more, Tommy checks in some good scores.

The other three players, who will tee off at 10 a. m., are A. S. Beyington, director of vocational education for the state board of education; the Hartford Golf club professional, Sid Covington, and Arthur B. McGinley, sports editor of The Hartford Times.

As part of his program this week in having Mr. McAuliffe demonstrate what handicapped men can do, E. P. Chester, the director of vocational rehabilitation for the state board of education, has arranged the golf match. In the interested "gallery" of state officials at the links Tuesday will be State Comptroller Frederick M. Salmon.

It is Mr. Chester's job to direct the work of rehabilitating handicapped men for a useful place in industry.

Tommy McAuliffe is appearing this week at the Capitol theater.

Rooftop Exhibition, Los Angles, CA 1940

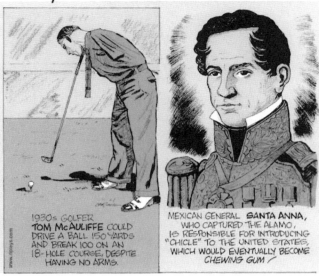

1930s GOLFER TOM McAULIFFE COULD DRIVE A BALL 150 YARDS AND BREAK 100 ON AN 18-HOLE COURSE, DESPITE HAVING NO ARMS.

MEXICAN GENERAL SANTA ANNA, WHO CAPTURED THE ALAMO, IS RESPONSIBLE FOR INTRODUCING "CHICLE" TO THE UNITED STATES, WHICH WOULD EVENTUALLY BECOME CHEWING GUM!

—By News Staff Photographer.

HARRY HINKKANEN   **TOMMY McAULIFFE**

McAuliffe, the world's champion armless golfer, visited Harry, 14-year-old boy who lost his hands in an accident last May, and gave Harry his first lesson in golf. He told Harry how to overcome obstacles in life, even though severely handicapped, as well as in golf.

The Author's Dad, Bob, tests out Tommy's concentration

THOMAS P. McAULIFFE

THE KING OF SPUNK

On September 13, 1901, eight-year-old Thomas P. McAuliffe ran into the road in front of his home at Eggertsville, N. Y. Tripping over a stone, he fell heavily and crashed his right temple against the outer rail of a street car line. He lay unconscious for several minutes and came to with the screech of grinding wheels in his ears. A massive flatcar, loaded with crushed rock, bore down on him. Instinctively, his head jerked back and his arms shot forward. Four steel wheels passed over both arms!

Little Tommy McAuliffe struggled to his feet—his arms dangling from his body by mere threads. He stumbled to his back yard. His aunt grabbed him, tied up both arms at the shoulder and saved his life. Tommy was carried on a chair to a hospital half a mile away. He remained there for two weeks and a day and has been on the go ever since.

Today, at 44, he shoots an 86 in the most exasperating game in the world!

1 In seven pictures, Tommy demonstrates his armless drive. He grips the club with his neck, right shoulder and cheek.

2 Tommy's drives average 160 yards. With his irons he covers between 75 and 100 yards. He carries 17 clubs and uses them all.

3 He learned to play golf as a caddy Buffalo Country Club, Buffalo, N. Y. H played in almost every country in the

4 Tommy's best score for eighteen holes is 86. He has handed in that score four times on courses measuring over 6000 yards.

5 In 1932 he played 262 rounds on 262 different courses in the U. S. and Canada with an average score of 92½ strokes per round.

6 An exhibition golfer in the summer, To turns lecturer, writer and promotion ager during the winter months.

FORE! Golfers! FORE!

Clear The Fairway

for the one and only

TOMMY McAULIFFE

World's Champion Armless Golfer

NOW FEATURED AT THE

PARAMOUNT

THEATRE

In the Sparkling Stage Show

"STITCH IN TIME"

In His Own Inimitable Act

The General Public Is Invited To View

TOMMY McAULIFFE

TODAY at 4:30 P. M.	on the main floor of our store in a demonstration of Golf Shots—unique and orthodox!!	TODAY at 4:30 P. M.

McAuliffe will inspire every Golfer to better play. See him DRIVE....
watch him APPROACH.... view him as he PUTTS.... and then stare at
him as he goes through a repertoire of Trick Shots........he's a wonder!

What McAuliffe Does With NO ARMS You Should Do With Two!

ONE ARM AGAINST NONE

JOSEPH SWEENEY   **TOM McAULIFFE**

The strangest golf match ever beheld—a sight that would have gladdened the hearts of the Geneva disarmament conference—was witnessed on the Franklin Park links today when Joseph Sweeney, Boston's famous one-armed golfer, played Tom McAuliffe, the no-armed golf marvel, who is showing audiences at the Metropolitan this week how he plays without hands.

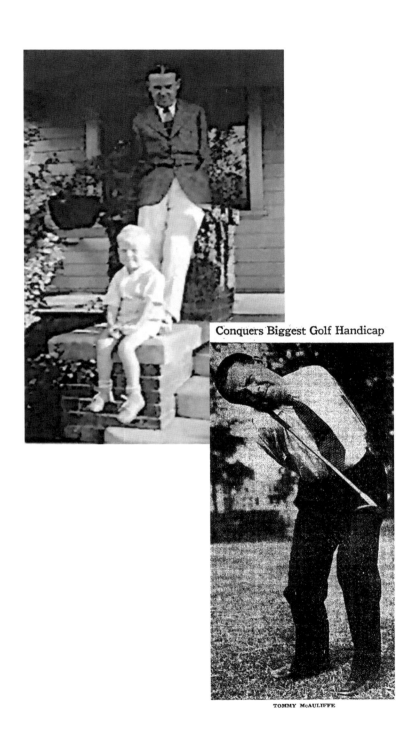

Conquers Biggest Golf Handicap

TOMMY McAULIFFE

Golfing Tips From An Expert

Brice Gamble (center) and Art Lockard (right), Ad club golfers who have been off their game all season, take a few tips from Tommy McAuliffe, armless golfer who is appearing at the Paramount theater.

Acknowledgments

Kissimmee Country Club, Florida

The USO

The United States Congress - Master at
Arms Disabled American Veterans

Buffalo New York Sports Association United
Press International

ABC, NBC, CBS

The New York Times

Ripley's Believe It or Not, Inc.

The McAuliffe Heritage Center, Ireland

Plum Hollow County Club, Southfield MI

Wally Fisher

Pat Noel

Thad Tinney

Jeanne Tinney Adams

Diane Bockelman

Copy Editor Nevvie Gane

Cover Design by Gene Buban